10649823

Wisdom
to
Grow On

Wisdom
to
Grow On

Incredible Letters and Inspiring Advice for
Getting the Most Out of Life

by Charles J. Acquisto

RUNNING PRESS
PHILADELPHIA · LONDON

9   8   7   6   5   4   3   2

Digit on the right indicates the number of this printing

Library of Congress Control Number: 2005932575

ISBN-13: 978-0-7624-2616-4

ISBN-10: 0-7624-2616-0

Cover design by Bill Jones

Interior design by Jan Greenberg

Text and organization by Nick Yost

Edited by Deborah Grandinetti

Typography: Century Old Style, bulldog, and DINEngschrift

Publisher's Note: All quotes and letters within are used by permission. All participants held the positions and job titles as noted at the time of correspondence.

This book may be ordered by mail from the publisher. Please include $2.50 for postage and handling.

But try your bookstore first!

Running Press Book Publishers

125 South Twenty-Second Street

Philadelphia, Pennsylvania 19103-4399

Visit us on the web!

www.runningpress.com

Contents

Acknowledgments

To my beautiful wife, Terri, who has undertaken an incredible life's journey with me. I could not ask for a better friend to accompany me on this exciting, uncharted trip.

To my son and firstborn, Nicholas, whose first breath of life became the single, greatest moment in my history and changed my world forever.

To my son Matt, for allowing me to be Dad. You are a great role model for your younger siblings.

To my daughter Gabrielle, who is my beautiful muse and one powerful princess.

For showing me by example the ABC's of parenthood, thank you Mom and Dad. A son could not wish for better folks. You gave me life's greatest gift: unconditional love.

To my in-laws, Don and Carole, for the wonderful time and love you give to our family.

To my literary agent Ted Weinstein, for taking a chance on a rookie with no book publishing experience and demanding nothing but the very best from me.

To reporter Joan Morris, for giving life to this story.

To all the letter writers to Nicholas, whether published or not in this book. I once again thank you for making a father's dream gift to his son come true.

To Jennifer Kasius of Running Press for believing in this book and for my editor Deborah Grandinetti for guiding me through this exciting process.

To Good Tidings Foundation founder Larry Harper, for quietly serving as a remarkable role model, giving and making a positive difference in the world every day. I am not sure if you have seen the world, but I sure want the world to see you.

Finally, to my Catholic School teachers who patiently taught me how to properly write a letter, an art form that is sadly becoming lost in the fast-paced, electronic age.

Introduction

On June 13, 2001, the greatest moment of my life occurred: the birth of my firstborn, Nicholas James Acquisto. On this happy occasion, I realized that my heaping plate of joy came with a hefty side helping of responsibility.

Over the course of the next few weeks, I thought about all that life had in store for Nicholas and how best to prepare my boy for what would lie ahead. Having a journalism background and a love of writing, I decided to celebrate Nicholas' first year of life on Planet Earth with a unique undertaking: I would write letters to successful people from all walks of life and ask them to share their definitions of success, love, and happiness.

In July 2001, I began writing letters during my lunch hour. Using my computer, I scoured the Internet for viable addresses of successful people. It is amazing what one can find on the Internet. My goal was to write at least one letter for each day of Nick's first year in order for him to have at least 365 responses. I quickly realized that obtaining 365 return letters out of 365 attempts was about as realistic as my winning a Pulitzer Prize, an Oscar, and the million-dollar lottery in the same year—less than none. Making up for lost time and long odds, I began mailing 15 or 20 letters at a time during the summer of 2001.

Each mailing that I sent contained a cover letter from me explaining my mission, four questions to be answered, a blank

"Dear Nick" letter for the respondent to write on, a self-addressed, stamped envelope, and a thank-you letter from Nicholas with his baby photo to show that Yes, Virginia, there is a Nick. I told no one of my plan for two reasons: I wanted the gift to be a surprise on Nick's first birthday and I was not sure anybody would write back to him.

By late July, replies began filtering into my law office. The first was from former President George H.W. Bush. His letter to Nick came in an 8 x 11 envelope complete with a rice paper protective cover, a nice touch that showed Bush's love of letters. Oprah Winfrey, the former Baltimore WJZ-TV *People Are Talking* co-host who parlayed a Chicago talk show into a billion-dollar enterprise, quickly responded. Golfing great Phil Mickelson was the first to actually write a response by hand on the "Dear Nick" letter that I had provided.

Like a child tasting sugar for the first time, I was instantly addicted. Nick's birthday present was coming to fruition. More addresses and more letters meant more responses for him.

I soon learned that senior respondents, who enjoy old school communication, found writing responses on my cover letter to be easiest, especially since I had left so darn much room by double- and quadruple-spacing it. While I appreciated the advice I received this way from Hollywood and athletic greats, I quickly expanded the cover letter, eliminated the extra space in the paragraphs, and filled the bottom portion with lengthy handwritten notes to let the recipients know why I was writing to them.

Then came September 11, 2001, which was quickly followed by the great anthrax scare that effectively shut down or quarantined much of the U.S. Postal Service's East Coast delivery. Hundreds of my letters were circulating or already sitting in piles waiting to be opened by assistants or family. I worried that fear of anthrax would put the kibosh on Nick's birthday present. I began to send some letter requests by electronic mail. Many people responded in kind and while I was elated by their response, I found that e-mail could not capture the personality conveyed by a handwritten letter.

To my utter amazement, the pre-anthrax-scare letters kept coming back to Nick with handwritten responses. A couple of letters—one from Burbank, California and another from Massachusetts—were unsigned. While it was fun to try to guess who wrote them, the suspense was killing me, so I started to write the recipients' initials on the reverse side of the self-addressed, stamped envelopes before I sent them.

A couple of letters came back with something extra. The late singer Hank Ballard, who sang one of Nick's first favorites, "Finger Poppin' Time," sent a box with a two-page letter to me, a letter of advice to Nicholas, autographed photos, three greatest-hits compact discs, and video tapes from his PBS performance with his group, The Midnighters. The box had more than fifty 37-cent stamps on it and became an additional collector's item for Nick.

When Nick's birthday rolled around on June 13, 2002, I filled two boxes with binders containing copies of the letters. My wife, Terri, was consumed with curiosity on our drive to my in-laws for the small party for Nicholas. What on earth could I have in two office supply boxes that any one-year-old boy would be interested in?

At the party, I waited until Nick and his Grandpa Don, who shares Nick's June 13 birthday, had opened their gifts before allowing a sleepy Nick to pop open the boxes. Nick's interest lasted nanoseconds and his attention returned to taking a nap on his colorful Gymboree parachute. But his great-grandmother Elaine fell instantly in love with the gift, leafing through the letters and seeing the names of the stars, authors, politicians, and athletes she had grown up hearing and watching. Later, Terri was moved to tears and called her friends to tell them of the special gift to Nick.

Most sane people would have called it quits at that point. But the following Monday I was back at my desk jotting down names of more potential letter recipients. I even began faxing requests to successful people when I was unsure whether their addresses were valid.

It was about this time that Virgin Records and airline founder Richard Branson wrote back to Nicholas and said he hoped we would have good luck with the book. Branson's confusion with perhaps another letter proposal inspired me. While wonderful Nicholas had volumes of letters full of loving advice on achieving success and happiness in life, would it not be better if they could be available to the public? I had already shared many of the letters with family and friends. Perhaps even better than merely being posted on an Internet website, these personal letters to Nick could be published in a book to benefit a wonderful cause.

I contacted Larry Harper, founder of the San Francisco Bay Area's Good Tidings Foundation, and asked if he would mind if I used my book of letters to raise money for the organization he had started in his garage in 1995. Any money generated from the book's sales would go to the foundation to help with its numerous projects for Bay Area youth. Larry agreed and wished me lots of luck on my publishing journey.

After sending a few letters to publishers and e-mails to literary agents, I began learning what a difficult path I was undertaking. One rejection after another piled up on my desk. I was in dire need of publicity to help illustrate my idea. *Contra Costa Times* features reporter Joan Morris came to the rescue with a telephone call to my office asking if I would tell the story. A few weeks later, Joan's article about Nick's letters landed in our driveway. It was surreal to see Nick's picture staring up at me from the top of the newspaper's front page.

By the summer of 2004, Nicholas' story had been published in Knight Ridder newspapers across the country. A major Alberta, Canada radio station talk show host called for a 15-minute interview. The media coverage helped gain literary agent Ted Weinstein's interest in the book project.

If anyone believes that Nick's letters were ever intended to be more than a birthday present when I conceived this project, I can lay that notion to rest by relating my next adventure. Ted's first instruction was, "Make sure to get releases from everybody who wrote you a letter." Yes, nearly three years after the letters began to arrive, he was asking me to track down each sender and obtain a release just in case we secured a book deal. There was no guarantee that we would. Most of the addresses I had used were either lost or no longer valid. This was a monumental task.

To my surprise, nearly 95 percent of the letter writers who I was able to reach again were willing to release their personal letters for publication. They had initially written to Nick with the understanding that their letter would simply be part of my birthday gift to my son, and nothing more. A couple of writers wished to make changes in their correspondence. Many sent best wishes. A handful requested copies of the book when published. I even received a call from the White House legal team, which gave me the Oval Office's blessing.

I also needed to get releases from the letter writers who had passed away. To my amazement, releases from the deceased were easier to obtain than many from the living, thanks to their wonderful families and friends and the attorneys for their estates. The Internet and my fax machine made procuring many releases quick and easy. Those writers who decided not to participate often wrote or called with an explanation.

Now, four years after Nicholas was born and more than one

year since I undertook the book project, this collection reaches the public. Nicholas still does not understand the letters. But when we see someone famous on television, Nick often asks me if that person wrote him a letter.

I hope you enjoy reading and sharing these letters of advice, remembering that everybody can be a success in his or her own arena. It all depends on each person's definition of success. As this book shows, there are more definitions of success, love, and happiness than one can ever imagine.

Part I:

LESSONS FROM LEADERS

The difference between a successful person and others is not a lack of strength, not a lack of knowledge, but rather a lack of will.

—VINCE LOMBARDI, GREEN BAY PACKERS
LEGENDARY FOOTBALL COACH.

Exceptional achievers tend to have a lot in common. They generally are smart, tough, bold, well-educated, ambitious and willing to take risks. As they make their way through this rough-and-tumble world, they learn a lot about themselves, a lot about human nature, and a lot about what it takes to reach the top. It is no coincidence that those who make it to positions of prominence often get involved in, and enjoy success in other endeavors. And it is no coincidence that their experiences make them well-qualified to pass on valuable advice.

"ASK QUESTIONS ALL YOUR LIFE. IT IS THE BEST WAY TO LEARN."

— PETER UEBBEROTH, ex-baseball commissioner

"The 21st century holds bright promise and opportunity for you and your generation."

—PRESIDENT BILL CLINTON, 42ND U.S. PRESIDENT

"Give life everything you've got — don't look for the easy way out."

— GEORGE H. W. BUSH, 41st U.S. President.

Fight for a Cause Larger than Yourself

"I am passing along to you the words that inspire me to strive for success on a daily basis. This quote is taken from *Faith of My Fathers*: "Nothing in life is more liberating than to fight for a cause larger than yourself." With these words, I hope you too find the inspiration to succeed."

— U.S. SENATOR JOHN McCAIN

THE COMMONWEALTH OF MASSACHUSETTS
EXECUTIVE DEPARTMENT
STATE HOUSE   •   BOSTON 02133
(617) 725-4000

MITT ROMNEY
GOVERNOR

KERRY HEALEY
LIEUTENANT GOVERNOR

July 14, 2003

Dear Nicholas:

I hope that this letter finds you well. Your father has undertaken a special project, and his efforts reflect a love that is truly inspiring. I hope that you will always cherish the moments you share with family and friends, because you will experience no greater happiness than when you are with them.

The best advice that I can give you is to always put forth your best effort in school. School is a very important part of our lives. When you work hard in school, you can accomplish many great things. I hope that you will continue to read as much as you can, do your homework, and dream about doing great things.

Oliver Wendell Holmes, the former Justice of the Supreme Court, said, "We are the leaders of the whole stream of life. We lead it in the same sense that small boys lead a circus parade when they march ahead of it. But if they turn down a side street, the parade goes on." I urge you to march on the path of integrity, service, and compassion. When you lead in such a way, the parade will follow behind you.

Good luck in your future endeavors. I wish you all the best.

Sincerely,

Mitt Romney

"SET YOUR GOALS HIGH AND DON'T BE DETERRED BY THOSE WHO SAY IT IS IMPOSSIBLE."

—STEVE FOSSETT, Millionaire Adventurer

"Be proud of your mother! Look out for her when she is older."

—PETER UEBERROTH, FORMER BASEBALL COMMISSIONER

"REMEMBER, THERE IS A UNIQUE VOICE INSIDE YOU, NO MORE IMPORTANT THAN OTHER PEOPLE AND THE WORLD OUTSIDE, BUT NO LESS IMPORTANT EITHER. FOLLOW THAT TRUE VOICE."

— GLORIA STEINHEM, the country's best-known feminist writer and activist

"Always feel good about yourself and be kind to others. Life is a fun experience. Enjoy!"

— WALLY AMOS, Author and Founder of the "Famous Amos" brand

"TO BE SUCCESSFUL IN LIFE, MY ADVICE TO YOU IS TO ALWAYS BELIEVE IN YOURSELF AND BE A MAN OF ACTION. WORK HARD AND STAY TRUE TO YOURSELF."

— DONALD V. WATKINS, Billionaire Attorney

"LIVE EACH DAY AS IF IT WERE YOUR LAST AND BELIEVE IN YOURSELF."

— Richard Branson, Owner, Virgin Atlantic Airlines

STRAIGHT ANSWERS
TO THE FOUR QUESTIONS.

■ **GERRY SPENCE,**
ATTORNEY AND AUTHOR OF
HOW TO ARGUE AND WIN EVERYTIME

Q. *How can I be a success in life?*
A. Follow your passion.

Q. *What is the most important thing in the world?*
A. Health.

Q. *What is love?*
A. It is the fudge frosting on life's cake.

Q. *What is happiness?*
A. The cake

WILLIAM JEFFERSON CLINTON

December 21, 2001

Nicholas James Acquisto
Pleasanton, California

Dear Nick:

I am delighted to congratulate you
on the wonderful occasion of your birth
on June 13, 2001. Your arrival is a cause
for great celebration to all those who love
you.

You are blessed to be born during this
exciting time. The 21st century holds
bright promise and opportunity for you and
your generation. I wish for you a long and
happy life, with days filled with lessons to
learn, people to love, dreams to fulfill,
and an abiding hope that will see you safely
from success to success.

Sincerely,

Bill Clinton

GEORGE BUSH

July 30, 2001

Dear Nicholas,

On June 13, 2001, you arrived in this great, big, wonderful world. Welcome!

Already you are a lucky little boy, for you have a mother and a dad and a wonderful extended family who love you so much. Love counts a lot, and you will grow up with lots of love in your life.

As you look ahead to the challenges that life surely will present, keep in mind that there is much about which to be optimistic. The world is ripe with opportunity for those who work hard, get an education, and play by the rules.

Always do your best. Be a doer and not a critic. If you are fortunate enough to take something out of the system, put something back into it. Give life everything you've got -- don't look for the easy way out. Above all else, be yourself and have fun!

All the best to you, Nicholas, in the exciting years that lie ahead.

Sincerely,

G. Bush

". . . MARCH ON THE PATH OF INTEGRITY, SERVICE, AND COMPASSION."

— MITT ROMNEY, Massachusetts governor.

"Find out what you'd rather do than anything, and go for it."

—ELMORE LEONARD, NOVELIST

"Read books. Read books! READ BOOKS!"

— HERMAN WOUK, Novelist

Relationships
Are Paramount

"Upon achieving 'success' Nick, my hope is that you realize that which is most important—family and friends. Someday, when you have become successful in whatever line of work you choose, remember that more important than any material gains you've made or co-workers you've impressed is the love and strength your relationships have. . .

I truly hope you find that success is best measured by the relationships you have with family and friends and not by the possessions you've gathered along the way!"

—FRANK "CATCH ME IF YOU CAN" ABAGNALE

Our Ref: dg/150503/sk

15th May 2003

Nicholas Acquisto
C/o Charles Acquisto
5700 Stoneridge Mall Road
Suite 350
Pleasanton
CALIFORNIA 94588
USA

Dear Nicholas

What a wonderful idea of your fathers for a wonderful book.

My advice to you would be "Live each day as if it were your last and believe in yourself".

Best wishes to you and your family.

Kind regards

Richard Branson
Chairman
Virgin Group of Companies

"By learning as much as you can, caring for others, and reaching your full potential, you can make our world a better place."

—GEORGE W. BUSH, 43RD U.S. PRESIDENT

"Work hard and stay true to yourself."

— DONALD V. WATKINS, **Attorney/Investor**

"Love the Lord your God with all your heart and with all your soul and with all your strength. (Deuteronomy 6:5). If you put Christ in your forefront you will learn how to serve others. Go with God."

—U.S. REP. JIM RYUN

"Success is best measured by relationships . . . not by the possessions you've gathered."

— Frank Abagnale, founder and owner of a leading fraud protection company

"NEVER STOP LAUGHING."

— DAVE BARRY, Author/Columnist

"I've spent my life around professional athletes. The one lesson they've taught me that will be important for you to remember is to never give up! No matter how discouraging or hopeless your circumstances seem, if you can keep trying and persevering, you can succeed in the end."

—LEIGH STEINBERG,
ATTORNEY/NFL SUPER AGENT

PHILIP H. KNIGHT
CHAIRMAN OF THE BOARD
CHIEF EXECUTIVE OFFICER

October 10, 2001

Mr. Charles J. Acquisto
5700 Stoneridge Mall Road, Suite 350
Pleasanton, CA 94588
Attn: Nicholas James Acquisto

Dear Nick:

In addition to giving yourself the gift of education, the best advice I can give you is to make absolutely sure you are doing what you love to do. The rest will follow. That is how I got to be where I am now.

The words that have most impacted my life are those of an old college professor: "The only time you have to succeed is the last time you try."

I hope you grow up to be an enthusiastic NIKE supporter.

Sincerely,

Philip H. Knight

PHK/smj

Help Those
Less Fortunate

"Try and help people who are less fortunate. Try to set aside time to make a difference in the lives of people who are physically afflicted or victims of racism or otherwise can't help themselves. This will be an important legacy."

—LEIGH STEINBERG, ATTORNEY

November 28, 2001

Nicholas Acquisto
5700 Stoneridge Mall Road
Suite 350
Pleasanton, CA 94588

Dear Nick:

I am honored to be included in this thoughtful gift from your father.

I am passing along to you the words that inspire me to strive for success on a daily basis. This quote is taken from *Faith of My Fathers*: "Nothing in life is more liberating than to fight for a cause larger than yourself."

Nick, with these words, I hope you too find the inspiration to succeed.

With best wishes,

John McCain
United States Senator

JM/jw

"ALWAYS PUT FORTH YOUR BEST EFFORT IN SCHOOL."

—MITT ROMNEY, Governor of Massachusetts

"Make absolutely sure you are doing what you love to do."

—PHILIP H. KNIGHT, NIKE FOUNDER

"Be as good to your father as he is to you."

— WILLIAM F. BUCKLEY JR., **Author/Editor**

The Harder You Work, the Luckier You Get

Let me tell you my experience. From the time I was in the fifth grade and wrote a play I knew I wanted to be a writer when I grew up. So, for years and years, I read all kinds of books, trying to decide what kind I enjoyed the most. It turned out to be fiction, stories and books that come from the writer's imagination. I began writing when I was in college, knowing I would need luck to be noticed and finally published, and do you know what? The harder I worked the luckier I got. Now I've been writing books and movies for 50 years and there is nothing in the world I would rather do.

Find out what you'd rather do than anything, and go for it."

—ELMORE LEONARD, BEST-SELLING AUTHOR

THE WHITE HOUSE

WASHINGTON

December 12, 2003

Dear Nick:

Thank you for your letter. I am always pleased to hear from young Americans.

I encourage you, and all young people, to set high standards and work hard to achieve your goals. I also encourage you to learn more about our Nation and its history by visiting www.whitehousekids.gov or www.whitehouse.gov.

By learning as much as you can, caring for others, and reaching your full potential, you can make our world a better place.

Mrs. Bush joins me in sending our best wishes for your future success.

Sincerely,

George W. Bush

Part II:

THE ENTERTAINERS WEIGH IN

Hollywood has always been a cage. . . a cage to catch our dreams.

—JOHN HUSTON

Performers learn an awful lot about people because their success is irrevocably dependent on them. Whether they perform in front of live audiences, make public appearances, or appear in movies and on television, they capture—and require—a lot of attention. This interaction with the public—most of whom are strangers—provides entertainers with unique insights and an invaluable education about kindness and cruelty, good manners and bad. It also leaves them particularly well-equipped to offer insights regarding happiness and success.

"Welcome to a great lifetime. To be a success, be yourself. God makes us all different. The original is better than the best copies. Love is the most important thing in life. Love is unconditional surrender to another person or ideal. Happiness is being content with what you have."

—ERNIE HARWELL,
DETROIT TIGERS ANNOUNCER

"IT'S NEVER TOO LATE TO HAVE A HAPPY CHILDHOOD! BEGIN IMMEDIATELY TO GREET EACH DAY WITH JOYOUS ABANDON. AH, YOUTH! I ENVY YOU YOUR FUTURE AND WISH YOU WELL ON THIS, WELL, ONCE-IN-A-LIFETIME JOURNEY."

— KEN HOWARD, Actor

"For success in life, just be yourself. Most important: honesty, loyalty and family! Happiness should follow if you're true to yourself."

— JIM MCKAY, Sports Commentator

Comedic Productions, Inc.
SmoBro Productions, Inc.
Remick Ridge Vineyards
Smothers Winery
Smothers, Inc.
Chromakey Music (Ascap)
Zany Music (BMI)
Rave Music (BMI)
Enlight Music (Ascap)
Tomard Music (Ascap)
T&D Music (Ascap)
SmoBro Music (BMI)

September 17, 2001

Nicholas James Acquisto
c/o Charles J. Acquisto
Law Offices of Stephenson, Acquisto & Colman
5700 Stoneridge Mall Road, Suite 350
Pleasanton, CA 94588

Dear Nicholas:

To be a success if this world and enjoy it, remember three things: Love your neighbors, laugh a lot, and learn to yoyo.

Best wishes,

The Smothers Brothers

KNAVE PRODUCTIONS, INC.
6442 Coldwater Canyon Avenue • Suite 107B • North Hollywood, CA 91606
(818) 754-0351 • Fax (818) 754-0356 • e-mail: smobro1@aol.com
www.smothersbrothers.com

"TO BE A SUCCESS, BE YOURSELF."

— ERNIE HARWELL, Detroit Baseball Announcer

"Part of being successful is the person you are and the values upon which you place importance. Caring about other people and the community you are part of are among these in my opinion. Honesty with yourself and others is another trait I value. It's hard to be successful in any way if you are always trying to fool others and kid yourself in the process. Facing reality is sometimes painful but in the end you'll be better off than living in a fantasy world. I would also try to surround myself with friends who possess these qualities."

—**TERRY CASHMAN**, SINGER/SONGWRITER

Dare To Be Different

"Dare to be different. Don't be discouraged or put off some idea you may have by people saying that it hasn't been done before or that nobody ever did it that way. That's all the more reason to try. We wouldn't have automobiles or airplanes if somebody didn't dare to be different. Follow your heart. It is very important to be educated and knowledgeable, but sometimes your heart disagrees with your mind and very often your heart could be right. Be happy! Happiness is really not wealth or material things. There are so many unhappy and miserable rich people. Happiness doesn't cost anything, so anyone can be happy even if they have nothing. Laugh a lot and enjoy your friends, your family and whatever it takes to bring you pleasure —as long as you don't hurt anyone, or do anything that you wouldn't be proud of, or that would upset your family. You can be anything that you want to be. Always remember that, if you work hard enough and really apply yourself, then you can accomplish whatever you wish. Concentrate on your goal and don't let anyone dissuade you and you can do miracles."

— NORM CROSBY, COMEDIAN

"BE YOURSELF!"

— Don Rickles, Comedian

"FOLLOW THE COURSE OF STAYING TRUE TO YOURSELF, YOUR DREAMS AND GOALS."

— BOBBY VINTON, Singer

"Happiness comes down to how you feel about yourself. Your actions as you live your life will give you your answer."

— RED BUTTONS, Actor/Comedian

"FIRST AND FOREMOST, I WISH YOU A WONDERFUL LIFE. KNOW THAT SELF-RESPECT IS THE CORNERSTONE OF THAT LIFE. NO ONE IS BETTER THAN YOU ARE, SO FILL YOUR MIND, YOUR BODY AND YOUR SPIRIT WITH THE WORLD AROUND YOU."

—— HENRY WINKLER, Actor, Director, Producer

"Do what makes you happy, whether it's gardening, selling or writing. . . .If you do something that makes you happy, you'll work harder. The harder you work, the better you get. The better you get, the better you'll do. Success is bound to accompany happiness!"

—JIM DAVIS, CARTOONIST

"MAKE SURE THE FIELD YOU CHOOSE . . . IS THE ONE <u>YOU</u> LIKE BEST."

—— BILL KEANE, Cartoonist

STRAIGHT ANSWERS
TO THE FOUR QUESTIONS.

■ DOM DELUISE, ACTOR

Q. *How can I be a success in life?*
A. Do what you like to do!

Q. *What is the most important thing in the world?*
A. Your kindness to others

Q. *What is love?*
A. Something you give.

Q. *What is happiness?*
A. Being busy with the work you love to do

MISTER ROGERS' NEIGHBORHOOD

Family Communications, Inc.
4802 Fifth Avenue
Pittsburgh, PA 15213

September, 2001

Nicholas James Acquisto
5700 Stoneridge Mall Road
Suite 350
Pleasanton, CA 94588

Dear Nick,

It was good to get to know you from a letter that your father sent us. You are fortunate to have a father who cares so much about you. I hope you know that many people care about you -- now -- and as you grow. I care about you, too, as a television friend, and I'm looking forward to the time when you'll grow into watching our television visits.

One of my favorite quotations is from THE LITTLE PRINCE, by St. Exupéry: What is essential is invisible to the eye. To me, that says that what's inside us is what matters most of all. I hope that as you grow, you will appreciate the many wonderful things that are inside you and that you will try to look beyond what your eye sees and find the fine inner qualities in others.

All of us here in the Neighborhood send our very best wishes to you.

Your television friend,

412-687-2990 Phone • 412-687-1226 Fax • www.misterrogers.org • www.pbs.org/rogers

MISTER ROGERS' NEIGHBORHOOD is underwritten by Public Television Stations and the Corporation for Public Broadcasting.

"BELIEVE IN YOURSELF, AGAINST ALL ODDS, AND FOLLOW YOUR DREAMS. WHATEVER YOU CAN DREAM, YOU CAN BE."

— KELLY PRESTON, Actress

"DREAM BIG. ACT BIG."

— MITCH MILLER, Singer/Conductor

"Set your goals high, dream your dreams and may your "Impossible Dream" come true. Have a great, creative and loving life."

— JOHN RAITT, Broadway star

"Being successful can be thought of as becoming rich and living the good life—big house, big cars, just plain BIG!!! But to be really successful, I think, you must find a passion in your life and go for your dream—a passion that really fulfills you.

When it's all said and done, it's how much hard work and FUN you've had that can add up to a greater success than all the money in the world.

Enjoy your life, and smile a lot.

—**MARVIN HAMLISCH**, COMPOSER/PIANIST

"DO WHAT MAKES YOU HAPPY."

— **JIM DAVIS**, Cartoonist

Listen to Your Heart

"I am pretty young myself and so I am not sure how sound my advice is, but I believe that success in life comes from following your heart. You will know the answer to every question or crossroad that you encounter. Just listen to your heart It's a noisy world and the answer inside you sometimes has trouble being heard. But take the time to quietly listen and you'll never go wrong."

—PIPER PERABO, ACTRESS

"Success is a funny word, It can be defined in many ways by different people. I guess it depends on what your priorities are. For me, I've learned that, while financial success is great and empowering, it's not the most important thing. Finding out what makes you happy is the most important discovery you will make. If you wind up doing what your life tells you to do, you will be successful. I have spent my life in sports and music, the two things I love the most. I've been lucky for this to be my fate. No matter the field you chose, I hope that it's something you love. You'll find that your days will be spent more happily and you will have a feeling of fulfillment that few get to."

—**TERRY CASHMAN**, SINGER/SONGWRITER

"Always have pride. Give your best. Have FAITH! And think POSITIVE! Always set realistic goals. Have a good plan to achieve your goals. Chase your DREAMS!"

— DICK VITALE, **ESPN Basketball Analyst**

"It is wise to let life come to you. Don't chase after it! Be patient, be prepared and enjoy it. It will find you and it will be good."

—DICK ENBERG, CBS Sports Announcer

"Happiness is not only the key to success, but the key to a fulfilling life. When things don't seem to be going your way, change your focus on the negative to what has gone right in your life. Everything always passes eventually, especially if you have faith."

—NANCY O'DELL, ANCHORWOMAN

DON'T BELIEVE ANYONE WHO TELLS YOU THE UNIVERSE IS HOSTILE OR THE WORLD IS UGLY. YOU DON'T HAVE TO HATE ANYBODY OR FEAR ANYBODY. YOUR CHANCE OF A GOOD LIFE IS EXCELLENT IN THIS COUNTRY."

— HUGH DOWNS, Television Host

STRAIGHT ANSWERS TO THE FOUR QUESTIONS.

■ SHERWOOD SCHWARTZ,
PRODUCER

Q. *How can I be a success in life?*
A. Do the very best you can in everything you do. You owe that to others, and, more importantly, you owe that to yourself.

Q. *What is the most important thing in the world?*
A. Love!

Q. *What is love?*
A. A mixture of affection and respect.

Q. *What is happiness?*
A. Satisfaction that you've accomplished all you can for yourself and for others.

"SUCCESS IN LIFE COMES FROM HARD WORK, STRONG LOVE AND FAMILY. KEEP FAMILY CLOSE AND LAUGH. HAVE A GREAT LIFE AND BE KIND."

— LEA THOMPSON, Actress/Dancer

"Remember, you don't get anything for nothing. Behind all success is hard work."

— DICK VAN PATTEN, Actor

"BE VERY POSITIVE AND WORK HARD."

—NEIL SEDAKA, Singer/Songwriter

**"Work hard and never quit!
And don't let anyone treat you badly!"**

—TIM MATHESON, Actor

"LIFE IS TOUGH AND REQUIRES HARD WORK AND DETERMINATION IN ALL THINGS."

—KEN BURNS, Director

"Success is being personally satisfied with how you make your living because you've earned from work what others regard as strong and you've hurt no one else in the process. To achieve it, simply always make sure you've done your best, even when you can get away with doing less for the same level of compensation."

—KEVIN SMITH, DIRECTOR

Monty Hall
Defines Success

"Success is hard to define. To some, it is the accumulation of wealth. To others, it is to rise to the top of your profession, or how much acclaim you receive. To me, success is having climbed out of poverty to achieve enough in my lifetime to do the things I wanted to do —help my parents, help some relatives and friends, do things for my community and country, have a great and loving marriage, have children and grandchildren I adore. That is not only success, but happiness.

Love is having someone's arms around you who cares for you through good times and bad, who tells you by the warmth of a smile and a tender look in the eyes that you are dear to one another."

— MONTY HALL, GAME SHOW HOST

"A great career will never be more satisfying than a great family."

—NANCY O'DELL, Television Personality

"LISTEN TO YOUR MOTHER!"

—ANDY WILLIAMS, Singer

"Always love and respect your family!! Be true to yourself and follow your dreams!!"

—KIM DELANEY, Actress

51 WEST 52 STREET
NEW YORK, NEW YORK 10019-6188
(212) 975-4321

Dear Nicholas: April 24, 2002

One of the best pieces of advice I can give for the attainment of any measure of success is this: first, simply do the best job you can each day, and secondly, keep your eyes on the next step up the ladder. When I was on a newspaper, I wanted to be a press service reporter and, finally when I became a reporter, I decided I wanted to be a foreign correspondent. I worked on it and finally made it. Others have said it more graphically than this, but I'm convinced the real secret of success is to keep your eyes on the road immediately ahead. Do this and you will avoid pitfalls. You will also reach the big goals in life much faster.

On the other hand, I don't mean that you try to succeed at all costs. You don't build success on the bodies of your friends, nor do you commit acts against the laws of God or mankind. You can be competitive and still be a good person, for success is always more permanent when you achieve it without destroying your principles.

Respectfully,

Walter Cronkite

"There are no guarantees in life for being successful or anything else. But I can tell you that if you love and honor your mom and dad and if you show kindness to those around you, you'll be a success without really trying. Work hard and laugh as often as you can."

—TIM CONWAY, ACTOR/COMEDIAN

"IF YOU'RE HAPPY, YOU'RE A SUCCESS. THE MOST IMPORTANT THING IN THE WORLD—BEING NICE TO PEOPLE—WILL MAKE YOU HAPPY. LOVE IS WHAT YOU HAVE FOR YOUR PARENTS. HAPPINESS IS LOVING PEOPLE. TRY IT. YOU'LL SEE HOW HAPPY YOU'LL BE."

—DICK MARTIN, Actor

STRAIGHT ANSWERS
TO THE FOUR QUESTIONS.

■ ERNEST BORGNINE,
ACTOR/ACADEMY AWARD WINNER

Q. *How can I be a success in life?*
A. Study and work hard!

Q. *What is the most important thing in the world?*
A. You! For no one can live your life.

Q. *What is love?*
A. Sharing!

A. *What is happiness?*
A. <u>Knowing</u> that you shared.

"LOVE LIFE. BE GOOD. DO GOOD THINGS."

—Pierce Brosnan, Actor

"Mahatma Gandhi had a good idea: "You must be the change you want to see in the world."

—Jeff Bridges, Actor

"TO MAKE IT SIMPLE: JUST FOLLOW THE TEN COMMANDMENTS!"

—KARL MALDEN, Actor

"Fill your mind, your body and your spirit with the world around you."

—HENRY WINKLER, Actor

"The most important thing in the world is inner peace—peace of mind and feeling good about yourself."

— N E I L   S E D A K A ,   S I N G E R / S O N G W R I T E R

"TRY TO LOOK BEYOND WHAT YOUR EYE SEES AND FIND THE INNER QUALITIES OF OTHERS."

—THE LATE FRED ROGERS, best-known for *Mr. Rogers' Neighborhood*

"Always stay a hair behind the event, always see the whole picture in small and grand happenings in your life. Have a good life and look up the word "grace" in the dictionary when you are old enough —and let the definition be a positive guide for you."

—ROBERT DUVALL, ACTOR

"Happiness comes from being loved by others and giving love in return. Sometimes it's short-lived, so be optimistic! Hold on to the feeling."

—NEIL SEDAKA, Singer/Songwriter

28 JAN 2004

HI-YA,
NICK!

I'M HONORED TO JOIN THOSE
CELEBRATING YOUR BIRTH,
AND TO ADD MY VOICE TO
THOSE SHARING THEIR EX-
PERIENCES ON ACHIEVING
SUCCESS.

MY FAVORITE ADVICE TO THOSE
SEEKING TO ACHIEVE IS TO
KEEP THE FAITH. THIS HAS
BEEN ESPECIALLY IMPORTANT
TO ME, HAVING REACHED MY
GOAL (SYNDICATION) AT 40
YEARS OF AGE.

KEEPING THE FAITH TO ME
MEANS "STAYING THE COURSE"
ABSOLUTELY KNOWING THAT WHAT YOU ENVISION
WILL HAPPEN. THIS ALSO MEANS TO CONTINUE
PREPARING, STUDYING, PRACTICING, LEARNING
WHILE WAITING FOR YOUR MOMENT TO ARRIVE,
SO WHEN IT DOES YOU WILL BE TOTALLY
PREPARED.

I HOPE THAT SOMEDAY THESE WORDS, ALONG
WITH OTHERS (INCLUDING MY FRIENDS BIL KEANE
AND FRED ROGERS) WILL SERVE YOU WELL.
BEST Morrie Turner

STRAIGHT ANSWERS TO THE FOUR QUESTIONS.

■ JEFF BRIDGES, ACTOR

Q. How can I be a success in life?
A. Be love

Q. What is the most important thing in the world?
A. Love

Q. What is love?
A. A beautiful adventure

Q. What is happiness?
A. Wanting what you have

Believe in the Goodness of People

"You will grow up in what promises to be a most amazing and possibly a most frightening century.

Whatever does happen, believe in the goodness of humankind. Depend on the hope that man is basically good. Fight against evil. Stick to your principles and, above all, believe in yourself. I wish all the best for you, Nick, and for your generation. Try to make the world a better place."

—RITA MORENO, ACTRESS

"DO NOT TAKE A DAY FOR GRANTED!"

—LEAH REMINI, Actress

"In life take it all in, one day at a time!!"

—SID CAESAR, Comedian

"THESE ARE ONLY TWO THINGS YOU NEED TO BE AWARE OF AS YOU MOVE THROUGH LIFE AND CHOOSE YOUR LIFE WORK:

1). BE TRUE TO YOURSELF AND DO ONLY, AS EMERSON SAID, WHAT "INLY REJOICES."

2. PERSEVERE. LIFE IS TOUGH AND REQUIRES HARD WORK AND DETERMINATION IN ALL THINGS."

—KEN BURNS, Director

"A quote I like a lot! 'Never, Never, Never, Never, Never, Never, Never give up!' Winston Churchill said this. He was British Prime Minister during World War II. All the best."

—JACQUELINE BISSETT, ACTRESS

"DON'T GIVE UP!"

—DICK CLARK, TV Producer/Personality

"Hidden in every problem is an opportunity! That worked for me."

—BUDDY EBSEN, Actor

Advice to Nicholas James Acquisto

Dear Nick

1) How can I be a success in Life?

Believe in yourself. Hard work and honesty. Do not let anyone tell you that "you can't"

2) What is the most important thing in the world?

Your family. Your Integrity

3) What is love?

Complete respect and admiration for another.

4) What is happiness?

Happiness is overcoming obstacles in life, achieving your goals – knowing that you have always tried to do your very best with your life.

Enjoy your <u>life</u> to its fullest – do not take a day for granted!

All my love to you and your family!

Sincerely,

Leah Remini

Doing It
"Exactly" Right!

"Many things in life will appear to your eyes. While few things will appeal to your heart, pursue those things in life which appear to your heart!

Success in life is a matter not so much of talent and opportunity as of concentration and perseverance. The difference I see between failure and success is doing a thing 'nearly' right and doing it 'exactly' right!"

— JERRY LEWIS, COMEDIAN

"Don't shop for food when you are hungry."

—BUDDY HACKETT, Actor/Comedian

"My Aunt Margie wrote in my schoolbook,
Good, Better, Best
Never Let It Rest
Until The Good
Becomes Better
And the Better
Becomes Best.
Whenever I feel there's something I can't handle,
these words always come to mind."

— BEN E. KING, SINGER

"Follow your dream!
Don't take no for an answer."

—DORIS ROBERTS, Actress

"Don't be scared to take risks. You can do anything you want as long as you put your mind to it. Enjoy your friends and family. Be there for them and use them as your confidants as well. Smile a lot and be patient. Enjoy the simple things in life. Sleep in on weekends."

—SUMMER SANDERS, BROADCASTER/EX-OLYMPIAN

"AS YOU WILL HOPEFULLY FIND OUT ONE DAY, SUCCESS WON'T BRING HAPPINESS, BUT HAPPINESS WILL CERTAINLY BRING SUCCESS."

—JOE MANTEGNA, Actor

"Work with people that you like to be with and can trust."

—ART LINKLETTER, TV Personality and Author

Dear Nick:

And remember that your DAD
LOVES you! and GOD LOVES you!

LOVE, also—from ME.

STRAIGHT ANSWERS TO THE FOUR QUESTIONS.

■ **PHYLLIS DILLER,** COMEDIENNE

Q. *How can I be a success in life?*
A. Work hard and be honest.

Q. *What is the most important thing in the world?*
A. Kindness.

Q. *What is love?]*
A. Compassion for others.

Q. *What is happiness?*
A. Contentment.

"The most important thing in the world is an education. The more you learn the more successful you will be in your life."

—JOE BARBERA, Cartoonist/Creator

"With Bill Clinton and George Bush among your pen pals, how will you ever have time to consider a few lines scribbled by the likes of me? Pretending to be interested will be a first step in learning an important lesson —feigning humility after achieving success."

—BOB COSTAS, BROADCASTER

Buddy Hackett's Secrets to Success

"Learn to use the potty as soon as possible. Try not to complain about trivial things as soon as possible. Listen to your Mom and Dad, until you find someone wiser who loves you just as much.

Learn as much as you can about everything historical, geographical and financial!

Use your mind and muscles as much as you can.

Don't lie to anyone, even if it would make them feel better.

Try to earn your way in life at things you like to do. Smile! Don't be a wise guy! You can't demand respect, you can earn it. Don't shop for food when you're hungry."

— BUDDY HACKETT, Actor/Comedian

"You can be successful by not taking anything I've advised you to do."

—David Brenner, Comedian

"Keep the faith."

—MORRIE TURNER, Cartoonist

"WORK HARD AND LAUGH AS OFTEN AS YOU CAN."

—TIM CONWAY, Actor/Comedian

Bobby Vinton
Theatre

September 23, 2002

Nicholas James Acquisto
C/O Charles Acquisto
Stephenson, Acquisto & Colman
5700 Stoneridge Mall Rd. #350
Pleasanton, CA 94588

Dear Nicholas James:

At the request of your father, I am writing with what he hopes will be words of wisdom and advice on life.

Throughout time, everyone has searched for love, success and happiness. The answer is as different as there are people in the world.

Your father is an attorney, I'm a singer/musician, and my best friend is a barber. Yet, each of us has found happiness, joy and success in our chosen fields. Your father wants you to know what I think "......is the most important thing in the world?" The fact is, it doesn't matter what I think is the most important thing in the world; the answer is what is important to you? One year, it will be playing football, riding your bike or going camping. Then, it will be on to greater things like finishing school, getting a job, or falling in love. Are any of these things less important than the other?

If you remember to follow the course of staying true to yourself, your dreams and goals and keeping dear the good values and honesty, love and honor, of asking God's help along the way and occasionally remembering to thank Him, I have no doubt that you will be......successful, happy and loved.

Sincerely,

Bobby Vinton

"THE BEST ADVICE IS TO GROW UP AND BECOME AS SMART AS YOU CAN, SO THAT YOU WILL KNOW WHAT ADVICE IS GOOD WHEN YOU HEAR IT."

—LARRY GELBART, Comedy Writer

"Nicholas! Obey your father for 17 years!! Then go have some real fun!"

—BERKELEY BREATHED, Cartoonist

Dear Nick:

I've been giving valuable advice for years. No one has taken it yet. I am forced to conclude that I don't know what I'm talking about most of the time. So, my advice is to not take my advice. And if you can figure out how to do that, you will hear the sound of one hand clapping and become one with the universe. Or insane. Po-tayto, Po-Tah-to.

Scott Adams

Part III:

Every day is a new opportunity. You can build on yesterday's success or put its failures behind and start over again. That's the way life is, with a new game every day, and that's the way baseball is.

—BOB FELLER,
CLEVELAND INDIANS PITCHER

To most people who participate, sports are pretty much just fun and games, a way to stay in reasonable physical condition and a recreation to be enjoyed in spare time. To the truly accomplished athletes, however, sports are more than just games and often not much fun. Blessed with talent or not, the elite athletes know they could have never made it to the top without hard work, lots of hard work. A strong sense of discipline is required to master skills and a tough mental attitude is needed to overcome the setbacks that invariably occur along the way. And, all are acutely aware that time will erode their skills and that the fans are a fickle lot. No wonder, then, that athletes learn a lot about life's ups and downs, and are particularly well-suited to pass along valuable tips that might smooth the path for those who follow.

"LISTEN TO YOUR PARENTS! WORK HARD!
ALWAYS TRY YOUR BEST! FOLLOW YOUR HEART IN THE PURSUIT
OF DREAMS. I WISH YOU A LIFE OF HEALTH AND HAPPINESS."

—MIKE KRZYZEWSKI, Duke University Coach

*My advice is to have fun at anything you choose to accomplish.
Go about it in a passionate way and, remember, make a commitment and then go for it. Great work ethic, discipline, persist-
ence and an unyielding passion for success and enjoyment.
Good Luck."*

—JIM PALMER,
LEGENDARY PITCHER/BASEBALL HALL OF FAME

"THE BEST ADVICE I CAN GIVE IS IF YOU WANT SOMETHING BAD
ENOUGH YOU CAN DO IT. MY LOVE FOR BASEBALL, MORE THAN
MY ABILITY, IS THE REASON I'M IN THE BASEBALL HALL OF
FAME."

—**BROOKS ROBINSON**, Baseball Hall of Fame

"YOU CAN'T ALWAYS CONTROL WHAT HAPPENS TO YOU, BUT YOU CAN CONTROL HOW YOU REACT TO WHAT HAPPENS TO YOU. LEARN TO ACCEPT YOUR LOSS[ES] WITHOUT BEING DEFEATED."

—PHIL NEIKRO, Legendary Pitcher/Baseball Hall of Fame

"Realize your true value is being uniquely created rather than what we accomplish. Use your giftedness, be humble, have faith. Things that matter are connectedness with God, your family, putting others above self. Happiness comes from within. Peace and contentment bring joy."

—PAUL MOLITOR, BASEBALL HALL OF FAME

"All the best in the future. May your life be what you make of it—'All Good.'"

—Ferguson Jenkins, Baseball Hall Of Fame Pitcher

Focus on What You Can Control

"Most good advice or wisdom is usually passed down from someone who has gone before. When I was a rookie in 1948, Hugh Casey, a veteran Dodger pitcher, said this to me: 'Son, there are some things in this league you can't change—the weather or your day to pitch, the ball park you're pitching in and the umpire behind the plate. Don't concern yourself with these things you can't change. Work on what you have control of—throwing strikes, keeping your curve low. Stay in control of what you can and you will be a winner.' Now, Nick, you may not grow up to be a big league pitcher but, what ever you do in life, Casey's advice is the way to go."

—CARL ERSKINE #17,
BROOKLYN DODGERS 1948-1959

"IN YOUR QUEST FOR PERFECTION, REMEMBER THE THREE D'S:
DESIRE
DEDICATION AND
DETERMINATION."

—ANDRE DAWSON, Baseball National League Most Valuable Player

"My advice to you is very simple, but not easily achieved. Strive for credibility. Once (it is) achieved, your (levels) of peace and success will be as insurmountable as you choose (to make them)."

—DOM DIMAGGIO, Red Sox Great

"Success can be measured in the two ways: worldly or Godly. Worldly success is fleeting and superficial. You can get it in many ways. Godly success is lasting and you can get it in only one way. It is through the way of the greatest book ever written, the Bible. It's your choice."

—RALPH KINER, HALL OF FAME SLUGGER

May 30, 2002

Nick Acquisto
5700 Stoneridge Mall Rd
Ste 350
Pleasanton, CA 94588

Dear Nick,

Your dad wrote to me and asked me to share some words of advice with you. The best advice I can pass along to you is something that I learned from my father when I was very young. He taught me that there are two things you must do to succeed:

1) Show up every day.
2) Give your best in everything you do.

If you know you've given your best, even though you may not achieve the result you were looking for or that others were expecting, you will not have failed.

Discover what brings you joy and make it a big part of your life. Also, find a way to bring joy to others.

Surround yourself with people you love, people who love you and people you can learn from.

Remember that everyone you meet, however ordinary or extraordinary they may seem, has something to offer you-- a lesson to be learned, wisdom to share.

Nick, I wish you the best as you begin to explore all that life has to offer you.

Sincerely,

Cal Ripken, Jr.

"BE THE BEST YOU CAN BE WITH THE TALENT GOD GIVES YOU."

**—DICK GROAT, former professional baseball player
who was also a Duke University basketball star**

"There are no shortcuts in life. If you hustle with concentrated effort every day to a high goal, you can achieve everything you desire—but only if you do it with a strong mental frame of mind, a bigger heart than you think you have, and with a burning fire in your belly."

FRANK "HONDO" HOWARD, HOME-RUN HITTER

"ALWAYS REMEMBER TO GIVE EVERYTHING YOUR VERY BEST. BE
KIND TO OTHERS AND CONTINUE TO ALWAYS BE RESPECTFUL.
KEEP A SMILE ON YOUR FACE FOR IT WILL UPLIFT OTHERS
AROUND YOU. KEEP YOUR EYES ON JESUS AND ALWAYS GIVE HIM
THE GLORY AND PRAISE. GOD BLESS YOU."

—GARY CARTER, Baseball Hall of Fame

STRAIGHT ANSWERS TO THE FOUR QUESTIONS.

■ BOBBY THOMSON,
BASEBALL LEGEND

Q. *How can I be a success in life?*
A. Study hard in school, be a good listener, do what your parents tell you.

Q. *What is the most important thing in the world?*
A. Try to enjoy people, enjoy life.

Q. *What is love?*
A. Love, I think, needs respect, tolerance, kindness, accomplishment.

Q. *What is happiness?*
A. Getting out of bed with a smile on your face.

These questions require more time than I have to fully answer.

"Nick, I know that you are quite young, and don't understand what's going on in your young life. And as you grow older, and your wonderful parents explain to you the future of your life ahead, listen to them. And listen to yourself, what your future plans are, and how to approach all prospects of becoming a great citizen, someday a great father yourself. Listen to all people, and use your own judgment as to how it can better your life. Work hard and believe in Christianity.

—VIRGIL TRUCKS,
BASEBALL LEGEND AND ALL STAR PITCHER

"LIFE IS SHORT AS YOU READ IN PSALM 90 AND IT IS IMPORTANT AS WE WALK DAILY WITH OUR LORD."

—BOBBY RICHARDSON, former New York Yankees All-Star

"Be good, work hard, and you will succeed in life. Make sure you know who your friends are."

—ROY SIEVERS, Four-Time American League All Star and batting champion

"Try to get a good start in life. Obey your parents and study hard. Develop a strong body, mind and spirit. Learn how to do something well—play a sport and become a fierce competitor. Try to do the right thing most of the time."

—MONTE IRVIN, FORMER NEW YORK GIANTS STAR

"TRY TO THINK POSITIVE. YOU CAN ALWAYS MAKE SOMETHING BETTER BY THINKING POSITIVE. LIKE WHAT YOU WANT TO DO IN LIFE AND THEN PRACTICE AND WORK HARD AT IT AND YOU'LL BE A SUCCESS."

—BOBBY DOERR, former Boston Red Sox player

"Listen to your parents and teachers. They are the people who will help you the most. All the best,"

—FRED LYNN, FORMER Boston Red Sox and
American League Most Valuable Player

STRAIGHT ANSWERS TO THE FOUR QUESTIONS.

■ CHUCK BEDNARIK,
PHILADELPHIA EAGLES CENTER AND
LINEBACKER/FOOTBALL HALL OF FAME 1967

Q. *How can I be a success in life?*
A. Pray.

Q. *What is the most important thing in the world?*
A. Prayer and church.

Q. *What is love?*
A. Love is commitment.

Q. *What is happiness?*
A. Love brings happiness.

"If you know you've given your best . . . you will not have failed."

—CAL RIPKEN JR., Baltimore Orioles "Iron Man"

"If you want something bad enough, you can do it."

—BROOKS ROBINSON,
ALL-CENTURY THIRD BASEMAN

"Learn to accept your loss[es] without being defeated."

—PHIL NEIKRO, generally credited as
the best knuckleball pitcher ever

ATHLETICS

Department of Athletics
Andy Geiger
Director of Athletics

Room 224, St. John Arena
410 Woody Hayes Drive
Columbus, OH
43210-1166

Telephone (614) 292-7572
Telefax   (614) 292-0506

ADVICE TO NICHOLAS ACQUISTO

Dear Nick:

How can you be a success in life?
- Believe in your yourself and follow your dreams.

What is the most important thing in the world?
- To me it is the love of my family and my belief in God.

What is love?
- I believe love is all around us each day and it is different to each person.
  It cannot be described in words.

What is happiness?
- Happiness is also different to each individual. To me, it's the privilege to live life
  doing what makes me happy and having the support and love of my family and friends.

I'd like to close by offering these words that were offered to me by a Jr. High School
counselor. They have helped me throughout my entire life and I hope that they be of some
assistance to you in your life.

It's called the 3 D's:

Desire   setting goals for yourself

Dedication   committing yourself to achieving those goals

Determination   overcoming obstacles that are in your way

I wish you all the best that life has to offer.

Sincerely,

Archie M. Griffin
Associate Director
of Athletics

Heisman Trophy Recipient 1974 & 1975

AG/sm

"BE HUMBLE. HAVE FAITH."

—PAUL MOLITOR, Hall of Fame hitter

"Only a person who loves can be loved. Love means kindness, understanding, wisdom and respect. Incorporate those attributes in your thinking, and your life will be fulfilled with warmth and compassion. There will never be an emotion with true happiness unless you give your love so that you can receive love."

—AL ROSEN, FORMER AMERICAN LEAGUE
MOST VALUABLE PLAYER

"STRIVE FOR CREDIBILITY."

—DOM DIMAGGIO, Boston Red Sox star

STRAIGHT ANSWERS
TO THE FOUR QUESTIONS.

■ BILL SHARMAN,
BASKETBALL HALL OF FAME

Q. *How can I be a success in life?*
A. To succeed in life there is no substitute for HARD WORK!

Q. *What is the most important thing in the world?*
A. God, your health and family!

Q. *What is love?*
A. Sharing your feelings with others

Q. *What is happiness?*
A. To me, it is trying to help others.

"THERE ARE NO SHORTCUTS IN LIFE."

—Frank Howard, Home-Run Slugger

*"Keep a smile on your face for it will
uplift others around you."*

—GARY CARTER, HALL OF FAME CATCHER

"MAKE SURE YOU KNOW WHO
YOUR FRIENDS ARE."

—Roy Sievers, Four-Time All Star

"Only a person who loves can be loved."

—AL ROSEN, Indians third baseman

"FOLLOW YOUR DREAMS, ALWAYS STAY HAPPY AND TREAT OTHERS AS YOU WOULD LIKE TO BE TREATED."

—JOHNNY UNITAS, Quarterback

"Be the best at whatever you choose to do in life."

—RONNIE LOTT, Defensive Back

Evaluate Yourself Honestly

"Life is full of challenges and opportunities. One of the best ways to live a life that meets and defeats challenges, and takes advantage of your opportunities, is to focus on "measuring yourself."

It is possible to fool your parents, family, friends, teachers, business associates. But, the Golden Key is to never fool yourself.

In whatever you do, always evaluate yourself honestly and seek to satisfy your own personal standard of excellence. One way that I have read this philosophy described in a simple way is: 'When you stare into the mirror, be sure you respect and admire the person who looks back at you!'"

—TONY LaRUSSA,
REGARDED AS ONE OF THE FINEST
BASEBALL MANAGERS EVER

"As you grow older you will find the most important thing you have and will come to cherish is time. Use it wisely. More importantly, share it—as all those people did who took the time to share their thoughts with you."

—ROCKY BLEIER,
FORMER PITTSBURGH STEELERS STAR

"Enjoy sports as a game. Have fun and do your homework."

—BERT JONES, Baltimore Colts Most Valuable Player

"Nick! You are a big winner. You will score Big in Life. I am blocking for you. If you want to go to Syracuse University, tell them I am your godfather. May the best of your past be the worst of your future. Winner?"

—JOHN MACKEY,
BALTIMORE COLTS/NFL HALL OF FAME 1992

"Maximize your God-given talents by always giving an all-out effort. Then try to exceed that effort."

—JOHNNY LUJACK, Heisman Trophy Winner, 1947

"Advice is a hard thing to give, but it's been my experience that if you try to do your best every day good things will happen. Also approach things with a positive outlook and have some fun along they way. Enjoy what you're doing."

—J O H N   C A P P E L L E T T I ,
H E I S M A N   T R O P H Y   W I N N E R   1 9 7 3

"My Father was "A Great American." He gave me two pieces of advice in life. If I get a tattoo in the Marine Corp get it on the bottom of my foot. Also, he told me to pick my own friends and not let somebody else pick them for me."

— A R T   D O N O V A N ,   H A L L   O F   F A M E   L I N E M A N

God is the Key to a Successful Life

"As soon as you are aware of who and what you are, try to find out why you are. You were born for a purpose in life. Find out what it is. We are all created for a purpose; that is why you were made! <u>God made us all</u>. Since God made us all, even your mom and dad, you must know who God is. This means you must put God in your life and read the Bible, where all truth is. We (you) must learn <u>to love all people</u>, no matter what color they are. God tells us "<u>You must love one another!</u>"

May you have a long life filled with love and helping others. God is your key to a successful life!"

—LENNY MOORE, FOOTBALL HALL OF FAME

arnⓞld palmer

post
office
box
fifty-two
youngstown,
pennsylvania
15696

September 27, 2001

Dear Charles:

Congratulations on the birth of your son. I think the scrapbook idea is a good one and am happy to provide some advice for your son to read when he is older.

I think Nicholas will find life to be more enjoyable and fulfilling if he decides to follow the bits of advice below.

- Treat others as you wish to be treated.
- Courtesy and respect are timeless principles, as well as good manners.
- Knowing when to speak is just as important as knowing what you say.
- Know how to win by following the rules.
- Know the importance of when and how to say thank you.
- Never underestimate the importance of a good education.

Best of luck to you both.

Sincerely,

Arnold Palmer

"God is the light and He is No.1."

—HERSCHEL WALKER, Football Running Back

"It took me awhile in life to understand what has to come first. Please don't wait as long as I did. You are here for a reason. Fulfilling that purpose will give you a fulfilled life."

—RAYMOND BERRY, FOOTBALL HALL OF FAME

"Work hard, discipline yourself, have goals. Education is most important to success. Reach for the stars."

—GEORGE BLANDA, Football Hall of Fame 1981

"Keep your dreams as you grow older and never give up. Keep yourself around people who want you to succeed."
—Rudy Ruettiger, Notre Dame Legend

"BE THANKFUL YOU HAVE SUCH A CARING DAD. MANY KIDS AREN'T SO LUCKY. IT'S A GIFT."

—John Gagliardi, the most successful college football coach

"Always remember that "success" is a word that only comes after hard work in a dictionary."

—HERMAN BOONE, THE HIGH SCHOOL FOOTBALL COACH IMMORTALIZED BY DENZEL WASHINGTON IN *REMEMBER THE TITANS*

Character is More Important than Reputation

"Success comes through peace of mind in knowing you made the effort to do the best of which you are capable. Only you will know that and you must realize that which you are. Your character is far more important than your reputation, which is merely what you are perceived to be.

True love for one another and enduring peace between all nations in this troubled world are the most important things that we should endlessly seek.

Love is 1 for 13.

Love isn't love until you give it away. It is always consideration for others. It is doing for others with no thought of something in return.

True happiness does not come from material things which eventually get taken away, but from the things that can never be taken away —giving, loving, caring, helping, etc."

—JOHN WOODEN, FORMER UCLA COACH
REVERED AS ONE OF THE ONE OF THE GREATEST
BASKETBALL COACHES OF ALL TIME

JACK NICKLAUS

June 8, 2004

Dear Nick:

I think growing up is a lot harder for children today than it was when I was your age. You face more difficult choices and experience greater pressures than earlier generations. But I hope you will accept that challenge gratefully, because you live in a country of tremendous opportunities and prosperity. May you find what you love in life, work hard to achieve your dreams, appreciate the people who help you along the way, and always strive to live your life with integrity, fairness, and respect for others.

Best wishes,

"FOLLOW YOUR DREAMS."

—Johnny Unitas, Baltimore Colts

"May the best of your past be the worst of your future."

—JOHN MACKEY,
BALTIMORE COLTS TIGHT END

"BE HONEST."

—Chuck Bednarik, Philadelphia Eagles

"Believe in yourself and follow your dreams."

—ARCHIE GRIFFIN, Ohio State

"SET YOUR PRIORITIES IN ORDER."

—BOBBY BOWDEN, Florida State University coach

"Learn early in your life to say no—and mean it. Know yourself before passing judgment on others. Live every moment of your life as if it might be your last. And, lastly, always try to do the right thing, even if no one is watching."

— TOM WATSON, PGA STAR

STRAIGHT ANSWERS TO THE FOUR QUESTIONS.

■ GREG NORMAN,
BRITISH OPEN CHAMPION

Q. *How can I be a success in life?*
A. The way to be a success in life is to make a decision using good judgment and never look back.

Q. *What is the most important thing in the world?*
A. The most important things in the world are family and friends.

Q. *What is love?*
A. Love is the unconditional devotion to someone.

Q. *What is happiness?*
A. Happiness is doing the things you love to do!

"Success in life has nothing to do with possessions. It has everything to do with improving the quality of life for those around you. Making other peoples' lives more enjoyable will make you feel like, and be, a success."

—PHIL MICKELSON, MASTERS CHAMPION

"YOU WILL NEVER GO WRONG IF YOU TELL YOUR MOTHER AND FATHER YOU LOVE THEM EVERY DAY. YOU'LL BE OK WITH A DAD AND MOM LIKE YOU HAVE."

—LEE TREVINO, PGA Tour Legend

"You will never go wrong in life if every decision you make is predicated on, 'Would my mother and father be proud of me?'"

—KEN VENTURI, Golf Player and Broadcaster/Analyst

"Remember to respect your parents, study and work hard, and the good things in life do not come easily."

—HALE IRWIN, GOLFER AND ONE OF THE MOST DOMINANT CHAMPION TOURS PLAYERS EVER

"Follow your dreams!"

—MATT KUCHAR, former U.S. Amateur Champion

"KNOW THE IMPORTANCE OF WHEN AND HOW TO SAY THANK YOU."

—ARNOLD PALMER, one of the greatest golfers of all time

FLORIDA STATE UNIVERSITY

FOOTBALL

October 2, 2001

Mr. Nick Acquisto
5700 Stoneridge Mall Rd.
Suite 350
Pleasanton, CA 94588

Dear Nick,

I would like to give you some advice for your future:

Q: How can you be a success in life?
A: Set your priorities in order: 1.   God
                                     2.   Family
                                     3.   Others
                                     4.   Profession

Q: What is the most important thing in the world?
A: Faith, Trust, Commitment to Jesus Christ.

Q: What is love?
A: God is love.

Q: What is happiness?
A: The immediate happy response to an event. It doesn't last but joy
     does.

I hope you will keep these things in mind as you grow up and become a
young man.

Sincerely,

Coach Bowden

Bobby Bowden
Head Football Coach

National Champions–1993
National Champions–1999

Moore Athletic Center • P.O. Box 2195 • Tallahassee, Florida 32316
Phone: (850) 644-1465, 1 (800) 644-2548 • Fax: (850) 644-1356
www.seminoles.com

"STRIVE TO LIVE YOUR LIFE WITH INTEGRITY,
FAIRNESS AND RESPECT FOR OTHERS."

—JACK NICKLAUS, Golf Champion

"Live every moment of your life as if it might be your last."

—TOM WATSON, Five-Time British Open Winner

"THE MOST IMPORTANT THING IN LIFE IS YOUR FAMILY."

—PHIL MICKELSON, Left-Handed Golf Champion

"MY ADVICE WOULD BE FOR YOU TO LOVE AND HONOR
BOTH YOUR PARENTS ALWAYS."

—Byron Nelson, 1940s Golf Champion

"Happiness is doing the things you love to do!"

— G R E G   N O R M A N ,
T W O - T I M E   B R I T I S H   O P E N   W I N N E R .

"IF YOU ARE EVER A GOLFER—
PRACTICE, PRACTICE."

—Lee Trevino, PGA Tour Legend

Success Thoughts for the Day

Each day at practice we use one of the thoughts as our goals for that day. Perhaps you will find some that you like and will help you down the road of life. God bless you always.

- Our judgment is only as good as our information.
- All saints have a past and all sinners have a future.
- A simple test of my character is how I treat a person who can do absolutely nothing for me.
- Feed your faith and your doubts will starve to death.
- Don't make excuses. Your friends don't need them and your enemies won't believe them.
- Enthusiasm creates heroism.
- The will to win is not as important as the will to prepare to win.

—MORGAN WOOTEN,
HIGH SCHOOL COACHING LEGEND

"Remember to always give your best effort in all that you do . . .
To be successful, you must have confidence in your abilities."

— **RICK BARRY**, BASKETBALL
HALL OF FAME/BROADCASTER

'BE A GIVER AND NOT A TAKER. LOVE SOMEONE
MORE THAN YOURSELF."

—DAVE COWENS, Basketball Hall of Fame

"DO YOUR BEST WHEN NO ONE IS WATCHING!"

—Bob Cousy, Basketball Hall of Fame

Byron Nelson

778 Litsey Rd. • Roanoke, Texas 76262

August 30, 2001

Dear Nicholas,

     Your father asked me to answer a question to help you be a success in life. He obviously loves you a great deal, so you're blessed to have such a father. My advice would be for you to love and honor both your parents always, as the Bible promises if you do, you'll do well and have a long life. And also, you need to seek God, study his Word, and try hard to become as much like Christ as you can be.

               Sincerely,

               Byron Nelson

"Believe in yourself, listen to your parents and go to the best high school and college possible!! Oh, and my mom says to 'eat your veggies!'"

—CHRISTIAN LAETTNER,
COLLEGE BASKETBALL GREAT

"Everything in life happens for a reason, so accept it and get on with your life."

—RICK BARRY, Basketball Hall of Fame/broadcaster

"Remember to always give your best effort in all that you do."

—RICK BARRY,
FIVE-TIME ALL-NBA PLAYER

"FOLLOW YOUR HEART IN THE PURSUIT OF DREAMS."

—MIKE KRZYZEWSKI, Duke basketball coach

"Love isn't love until you give it away."

—JOHN WOODEN, COLLEGE COACHING LEGEND

"FEED YOUR FAITH AND YOUR DOUBTS WILL STARVE TO DEATH."

—MORGAN WOOTTEN, Famed high-school coach.

You Learn More by Listening

"After spending many decades on this Earth, I have learned many things. Listening to other people wiser than me is one example. You will learn many things listening, fewer things talking.

I was the youngest of eight children. Being the youngest often meant learning from mistakes as my older brothers and sisters corrected me on social behavior—saying thanks when someone gives you something, having respect for older people, and paying attention when corrected.

As a coach, I found my school background and college very helpful. In a moral ethics class at a Jesuit school the teacher would often emphasize: "One does not do a good act to have a good result." In coaching, it really helped as I told my players to abide by the school and conference rules. Do not cheat and break rules when recruiting. When we go into one's life we should always remember: Is it a good act you are attempting? In your professional life you will often face this issue, so don't do a wrong to get a good result.

Treat people, all people, as you would like to be treated. Be polite and respect other people as you would like to be respected. Money is not the answer to every problem and in itself will not bring happiness. Be a good son to your father and be a good father to your children."

—PETE NEWELL, BASKETBALL HALL OF FAME COACH

"BE A GOOD SON TO YOUR FATHER AND BE A GOOD FATHER TO YOUR CHILDREN."

—PETE NEWELL, Basketball Hall of Fame coach

"Always do your best and give more than you take—and have fun!"

—MARTINA NAVRATILOVA, Tennis Legend

"The most important thing in the world is a loving family because all the success in the world is nothing unless you have a family to share it with and a family that gives unconditional LOVE!!"

—SUGAR RAY LEONARD, BOXER

**"A winner never quits—
a quitter never wins."**

—BOB MATHIAS, Decathon Gold Medalist

**"ALWAYS BELIEVE IN YOURSELF
AND TRY REALLY HARD."**

—MIKE ERUZIONE, 1980 Hockey Captain

*"Take the time to appreciate all things.
Don't take anything for granted. And have a passion and
don't let anything stop you from dreaming."*

—JIM CRAIG, 1980 HOCKEY GOALIE

Sweat Plus Sacrifice Equals Success

"To succeed, you must have a positive attitude, high expectations to excel, and faith in God. Believe in the beauty of your dreams. Seize the moment! Achieve! Sweat plus sacrifice equals success.

The most important thing in the world is God, because he supplies you with strength, perseverance and wisdom. One can enjoy the blessings of a deep faith and face the difficulties of life with courage and confidence. Love is a positive emotion. Love is fondness, affection, sincerity, devotion, loyalty and reverence. "Love. . .always protects, always trusts, always hopes, always perseveres." 1 Corinthians 13:6, 7

Happiness is a feeling of satisfaction, pleasure, contentment, elation, gratification. Happiness lies in the joy of achievement and the thrill of creative effort."

—MARY LOU RETTON, OLYMPIC GYMNAST

"BE HONEST—TAKE RESPONSIBILITY— OR ELSE NOTHING ELSE MATTERS."

—HERB BROOKS, 1980 "Miracle On Ice" Coach

"Give more than you take—and have fun!"

—MARTINA NAVRATILOVA, PROFESSIONAL TENNIS CHAMPION

"Seize the moment! Achieve! Sweat plus sacrifice equals success."

—MARY LOU RETTON, Olympic Gymnast

"DREAM BIG. WORK HARD."

—BRUCE JENNER, Olympic Decathlon Gold-Medalist

"DON'T TAKE ANYTHING FOR GRANTED."

—JIM CRAIG, Olympic Hockey Goalie

"Always speak your mind."

—BRETT HULL, Hockey All-Star

Dear Nick:

The most important thing in life is your family. They are the people who care about you + will always be there for you.

Success in life has nothing to do with possessions. It has everything to do with improving the quality of life for those around you. Making other peoples' lives more enjoyable will make you feel like, and be, a success.

Sincerely,

Phil Mickelson

P.S. Enjoy your life and good luck.

Phil Mickleson, golf champion

Index
and
Celebrity Bios

ABAGNALE, FRANK: 28

Frank Abagnale is the founder and owner of a leading fraud-prevention company that is used by more than 14,000 financial institutions, corporations, and law enforcement agencies. He picked up his knowledge the hard way, by personal experience. Between the ages of 16 and 21, Abagnale successfully posed as a Pan Am airline pilot, a Louisiana attorney, a professor at a major university, and a pediatrician. Along the way, he cashed $2.5 million in fraudulent checks in 50 states and 26 foreign countries. Nabbed by the French in 1969, he served five years in French, Swedish, and U.S. prisons before agreeing to a work-release program with the U.S. government. He chronicled all of this in his bestselling book, *Catch Me If You Can*, which was made into a movie starring Leonardo DiCaprio.

ADAMS, SCOTT: 78

In creating his hit cartoon, "Dilbert," **Scott Adams** drew on his years of "humiliating and low-paying jobs" at a San Francisco bank, where he was held up twice, and later as a pseudo-engineer at Pacific Bell in San Ramon, California. Born and raised in Windham, New York, Adams earned his business degree at Hartwick College in Oneonta, New York and his master's degree at the University of California, Berkeley. In 1988, Adams sent off samples of his work to United Features Syndicate, which launched the strip in 1989 in 50 newspapers. Adams continued to work at PacBell for inspiration and a secure paycheck. In 1995, he left the company to run Dilbert's world full time. That includes the daily strip and dozens of books, including two Number One *New York Times* bestsellers. Adams also owns a vegetarian food company and co-owns two restaurants. Today, "Dilbert" appears in more than 2,000 newspapers in 65 countries.

AMOS, WALLY: 20

When **Wally Amos** appeared on the hit comedy *Taxi*, the cookie entrepreneur proved he could even make his dough on a television show. Born in Tallahassee, Florida, in 1936, Amos grew up in New York City with his cookie-baking aunt, Della. She inspired Amos to enroll at the Food Trades Vocational High School. That led him to working in the stock room at Saks Fifth Avenue and the mailroom at the William Morris Agency. Amos's eye for talent landed him a position as the first black talent agent at William Morris, where he attracted clients by sending them chocolate cookies and inviting them to come see him. He worked with singers Simon and Garfunkel, Diana Ross, Marvin Gaye, and Sam Cooke. Eventually he moved his family to Hollywood to strike out on his own, but he did not make it. So he went back to baking chocolate chip cookies. With financial backing from Gaye, Amos opened his first Famous Amos store in 1975 on Los Angeles' Sunset Strip. By the late 1970s and early 1980s, Amos was the king of the gourmet cookie world. In 1998, Keebler bought the Famous Amos brand and Amos began tackling the muffin market with a partner and a company called Uncle Noname Gourmet Muffins. It is now Uncle Wally's Muffin Company and its products are sold nationwide. Amos is also the author of several books and a public speaker who shares his insights on managing change and overcoming adversity.

BARBERA, JOSEPH: 73

With his creative partner, William Hanna, New York City-born **Joseph Barbera** created *Tom and Jerry* (1940), *The Flintstones* (1960-66), *The Jetsons* (1962), and *Hey There, It's Yogi Bear* (1963). The cartooning duo captured seven Academy Awards for animated shorts from 1943 to 1953. Barbera wowed audiences when Jerry the Mouse danced with Gene Kelly in *Anchors Aweigh* (1945). *The Flintstones* became television's first prime time cartoon series. Emmy Award winners for Barbera include *Huckleberry Hound* (1958-62) and *The Smurfs* (1981-1990). Among his other animation creations are *Top Cat* (1961), *Jonny Quest* (1964), and *Charlotte's Web* (1973).

BARRY, DAVE: 28

Humorist **Dave Barry** is the author of 25 books and a *Miami Herald*-based column, which was syndicated in more than 500 newspapers until he took a sabbatical leave in 2005. In 1988, one of his columns won the Pulitzer Price for commentary. In addition, two of his books were the basis for a television show, *Dave's World*, which starred Harry Anderson. He spends some of his free time on tour with the Rock Bottom Remainders, a rock band comprised of friends and fellow writers who, according to Barry, "are not musically skilled but they are extremely loud."

BARRY, RICK: 114, 116

After an All-American career at the University of Miami, in which he led the nation in scoring as a senior (37.4 points per game), **Rick Barry** captured Rookie of the Year honors playing for the National Basketball Association's San Francisco Warriors in 1966. Nearly 10 years later, Barry willed the underdog Golden State Warriors to a stunning upset of the heavily favored Washington Bullets with a four-game sweep in 1975. In between, Barry starred for the American Basketball Association's Oakland Oaks, Washington Capitols, and New Jersey Nets. Barry is the only player to lead the National Collegiate Athletic Association, ABA, and NBA in scoring. A five-time All-NBA First Team player (1966, 1967, and 1974-1976) and four-time All-ABA First Team selection (1969-72), Barry was named to the NBA's 50th Anniversary All-Time Team in 1996.

BEDNARIK, CHUCK: 89, 105

An All-American at the University of Pennsylvania, **Chuck Bednarik** played center and linebacker for the Philadelphia Eagles in a legendary 14-year career (1949-1962) that included his team's capturing the National Football League title in 1960. He's considered the last of the NFL's "iron men" because he played both offense and defense. Bednarik, who never earned more than $27,000 annually playing the game he loved, was selected first overall in the 1949 draft. In the 1960 title game, Bednarik played 58 of 60 minutes and made a game-saving tackle in the Eagles' 17-13 victory. In 1950, Bednarik received All-NFL recognition as a center. Although he regularly played offense and defense through the 1956 season, he gained most recognition as a hard-hitting linebacker. He was named All-NFL as a linebacker in 1951 through 1957 and again in 1960.

BERRY, RAYMOND: 101

Raymond Berry made himself a Hall of Fame player by bringing precision and perfection to the pass route. Berry, who wore special shoes to correct the fact that one leg was shorter than the other, constantly fought the odds. He did not even make his Texas high school team until his senior year, even though his father was the head coach. Teaming with Baltimore Colts quarterback Johnny Unitas, Berry emerged from obscurity in the Colts' 1958 National Football League title game win against the New York Giants. Berry finished with a then-record 12 catches for 178 yards. An average runner, Berry spent countless hours before and after practice running routes to within inches of the way the coaches diagrammed them in the playbook. Berry finished his career

(1955-1967) with a then-record 631 receptions for 9,275 yards and 68 touchdowns. Not bad for a 20th-round draft pick out of Southern Methodist University! Berry later coached the New England Patriots to their first Super Bowl appearance in a 1986 loss to the Chicago Bears.

BISSET, JACQUELINE: 66

Brunette beauty **Jacqueline Bisset** was raised in England and has worked with some of film's greatest directors, including John Huston, François Truffaut, and Roman Polanski. The 5-foot-7 Bisset starred opposite Steve McQueen in the hit flick *Bullitt* (1968), but wowed the critics as the lead character in Truffaut's Oscar-winning *Day for Night* (1973). America again took notice of Bisset in *The Deep* (1973), where publicity shots of her in a wet T-shirt began a whole bar contest craze. *Newsweek* magazine even went so far as to name her "the most beautiful film actress of all time." Other Bisset movies include Rich and Famous (1981), *Who Is Killing The Great Chefs of Europe?* (1978) and *Under the Volcano* (1984). As for comedy, Bisset proved herself up to the task in her 1989 film, *Scenes From the Class Struggle in Beverly Hills*.

BLANDA, GEORGE:

Not many National Football League players can lay claim to playing in four different decades. Yet for 26 seasons (1949-1975), **George Blanda** was known as instant offense, starring as both a quarterback and a place kicker. He was the most valuable player in the former American Football League during his 1961 season with the Houston Oilers. In 1970, he was also the most valuable player in the NFL as a member of the Oakland Raiders. Able to beat other teams with the power of his arm and his right foot, he finished his career with a record 2,002 total points. In five straight games for the Raiders in 1970, Blanda tossed or kicked the go-ahead points in each game's waning seconds, netting four wins and a tie. Blanda, who also played for the Chicago Bears (1949, 1950-58) and Baltimore Colts (1950), threw for 26,920 yards and 236 touchdown passes before retiring at the age of 48. Blanda was enshrined in the Football Hall of Fame in 1981.

BLEIER, ROCKY: 97

After a football career at Notre Dame, **Rocky Bleier** was drafted in the 16th round by the lowly Pittsburgh Steelers in 1968. The following year, the fullback was sent to Vietnam, where he was shot in the left leg and a grenade exploded under his right foot. He returned to the Steelers in 1971, underweight and still feeling the effects of his injuries. He was used sparingly and was twice waived by coach Chuck Noll. But he persevered and managed to work his way back onto the team. A summer training program in 1974 brought his weight back to 212 pounds, and he made it into the starting lineup, specializing in short-yardage situations. In 1976, Bleier rushed for 1,036 yards (14-game schedule, 4.7-yard average per carry) and caught 24 passes. He retired from football in 1980. Bleier's story was turned into *Fighting Back*, a television movie starring actor Robert Urich.

BOONE, HERMAN: 102

An assistant coach since 1969, **Herman Boone** was named the first black head football coach at Alexandria, Virginia's newly integrated T.C. Williams High School in 1971 over a popular white coach, William Yoast. He faced the unenviable task of bringing cohesion to diverse coaching staff and players at a time of racial tension. Coach Boone, with Yoast as his assistant, brought the team together to amass an amazing 13-0 record, a Virginia state championship, and a national number two ranking. The T.C. Williams football squad was even credited with bringing unity to the city of Alexandria. That magical 1971 season was immortalized in the film *Remember the Titans*. Prior to coming to T.C. Williams, Coach Boone chalked up a 99-8 football record from 1961 to 1969 at E.J. Hayes High School in Williamson, North Carolina. One of 12 children, Boone knew from an early age that he wanted to teach and coach in order to reach youngsters and motivate future generations to accomplish their dreams.

BORGNINE, ERNEST: 58

Two of **Ernest Borgnine's** most famous roles have involved life at sea. In the television hit *McHale's Navy* (1962-1966), Borgnine displayed his comedic timing as the beleaguered Captain McHale. Later, Borgnine stood out in an all-star cast in the ocean liner disaster movie *The Poseidon Adventure*. Born Ermes Effron Borgnine in 1917, the future Hollywood star joined the Navy in 1935 and served for 10 years. Upon discharge, Borgnine fell in love with acting, working from bit stage parts to a small role in the Broadway comedy *Harvey*. In 1953, Borgnine struck gold by landing the Fatso Judson role in the blockbuster movie *From Here to Eternity*. Borgnine captured the Academy Award as best actor for his role as a sympathetic butcher searching for love in *Marty* (1955). Borgnine continued to bounce back and forth between film and television over the next four decades, including roles in *The Dirty Dozen* (1967), *Legend in Granite: The Vince Lombardi Story* (1973), and NBC's sitcom, *The Single Guy* (1995).

BOWDEN, BOBBY: 106, 110

Bobby Bowden is the winningest coach in the history of Division I-A, the big league of intercollegiate sports. As of press time, Bowden had racked up 351 wins, 102 losses, and four ties in 39 years. Bowden, who directed Florida State to national titles in 1993 and 1999, began his career at his alma mater, Samford University in Birmingham, Alabama (31-6 record), in 1959; he moved to West Virginia (42-26 record) in 1970 and took the helm in Tallahassee in 1976. Florida State had been to only eight bowl games in 29 years prior to Bowden's arrival and had won just four games in the previous three seasons. In 2005, the Seminoles played in their 26th bowl game of the Bowden era, topping off an 8-3 season with a 30-16 win over West Virginia at the Gator Bowl. His bubbly personality has landed him walk-on parts as himself on television shows, including Seminole alumnus Burt Reynolds' Evening Shade. As a father, Bowden can proudly lay claim to watching two of his sons, Tommy and Terry, become successful college head coaches at Clemson and Auburn, respectively. Bowden has co-written the best-selling book, *The Bowden Way*, with oldest son Steve.

BRANSON, RICHARD: 20, 26

Airline mogul and world adventurer **Richard Branson** first achieved fame with his Virgin Records label. Today, he owns numerous enterprises under the Virgin name, most notably Virgin Atlantic Airways, and has a multi-billion-dollar fortune. Branson's Virgin label encompasses everything from music and an airline to soft drinks, bridal gowns, train service, and a mobile phone network. An adventurer who has made several unsuccessful attempts to circumnavigate the world in a hot-air balloon, he has, however, completed record-setting balloon trips across the Atlantic and Pacific oceans. In 1994, he started a space tourism company. He plans to take tourists into suborbital space in the SpaceShipOne craft, which in 2004 made the first privately financed human space flight.

BREATHED, BERKELEY: 77

Berkeley Breathed is best known for the comic strip, "Bloom County," which featured Opus the Penguin and Bill the Cat. The strip earned him a Pulitzer Prize in 1987. "Bloom County" appeared in 1,200 newspapers around the world until he retired it in 1989. It was replaced by the Sunday-only cartoon, "Outland," which ran from 1989 until 1995. Eight years later, he reintroduced Opus in a Sunday-only cartoon. Breathed has also produced five children's books, a gift and ensemble collection, and drawings for the cartoonist character in the movie, *Secondhand Lions*.

BRENNER, DAVID: 75

Tonight Show veteran **David Brenner**, who appeared a record 158 times and hosted the highest-rated show when he filled in for legendary Johnny Carson, can take any mundane subject and find the humor in it. Four HBO comedy specials and five humor books, including his best-seller *Soft Pretzels with Mustard*, highlight Brenner's versatile résumé. Prior to conquering the stand-up world, Brenner was a successful writer/producer/director of 115 television documentaries that earned more than 30 awards, including an Emmy. It's easy to see why the likeable Brenner was voted class president and class comedian every year from fourth grade through high school graduation.

BRIDGES, JEFF: 59, 63

Actor **Jeff Bridges** has won Academy Award nominations for *The Last Picture Show*, *Thunderbolt and Lightfoot*, *Starman*, and *The Contender*. He also starred as photographer Jack Prescott in *King Kong*. Bridges is son of the actor, Lloyd, and brother of the actor, Beau. His résumé highlights include performances in *Tucker*, *The Fabulous Baker Boys*, *The Fisher King*, and *Seabiscuit*. He has also appeared in cult hits such as *The Big Lebowski* and *Rancho Deluxe*. Toss in Bridges' photography skills (books, exhibits), sculpting touch, a part-time music gig, and his founding of End Hunger Network and you end up with one well-rounded artist.

BROOKS, HERB: 122

Herb Brooks was architect of the "Miracle On Ice" as head coach of the United States 1980 gold medal Olympic hockey team. He guided an unlikely group of handpicked college kids to a win over the Soviet Union and, finally, to victory over Finland. When talking about how he chose players, Brooks liked to say he looked for the ones who felt that the name on the front of their jerseys was more important than the name on the back. After the Lake Placid Winter Olympics, Brooks coached the New York Rangers from 1981 to 1985, reaching the 100-victory mark faster than any other coach in franchise history. He also coached the Minnesota North Stars (1987-1988), the New Jersey Devils (1992-1993), and the Pittsburgh Penguins (1999-2000). He had a National Hockey League career coaching record of 219-222-66. Brooks played hockey at the University of Minnesota and made the U.S. Olympic team in 1964 and 1968. He became hockey coach at Minnesota in 1972 and guided his teams to National Collegiate Athletic Association

Division 1 championships in 1974, 1976, and 1979. He led the 2002 U.S. Olympic hockey team to a silver medal. In 2003, Brooks died at the age of 66 in a car accident several months before release of the movie *Miracle*, which celebrated the stunning 1980 upset victory.

BROSNAN, PIERCE: 59

"Bond. James Bond." For many, **Pierce Brosnan's** image will be forever linked to Agent 007, the famed hero of movies based on the novels of British author Ian Fleming. But the Irish-born actor first burst into America's consciousness on the hit television show *Remington Steele*. Fittingly, Brosnan claims the very first film he remembers seeing is *Goldfinger*, which starred Sean Connery as 007. Because of his contract playing Remington Steele, he was initially prevented from taking the Bond role from Roger Moore in 1986. That all changed in 1994, when he made the first of four James Bond films. A father of five, Brosnan rebounded from the difficult loss of his first wife Cassandra to cancer in 1991 to star in such hits as *Mrs. Doubtfire* (1993), *The Thomas Crown Affair* (1999), and his final James Bond film, *Die Another Day* (2002). Brosnan, who married Keely Shaye Smith in 2001, was voted *People* magazine's "Sexiest Man Alive" in 2001 and became a U.S.

citizen in 2004.

BUCKLEY, WILLIAM F., JR.: 32

William F. Buckley, Jr. founded National Review, a conservative opinion journal, in 1955 and served as editor-in-chief until 1990. He became widely known as host of the Emmy Award-winning television program, Firing Line, from 1966 until 1999. He is the author of 40 books, including *God and Man at Yale*, *Up From Liberalism*, *Cruising Speed*, *Let Us Talk of Many Things*, and *The Fall of the Berlin Wall*.

BURNS, KEN: 52, 65

Documentary filmmaker **Ken Burns** turned PBS into must-watch television with compelling series such as *The Civil War* (1990), *Baseball* (1994), and *Jazz* (2001). Blending narrated voices with still photography, Burns elevated the genre of documentaries to a whole new entertainment level. *The Civil War* became the first documentary to gross more than $100 million. Even the coffee table companion book sold 700,000 copies. Burns first gained notice with the 1981 Oscar-nominated *Brooklyn Bridge*. Burn's *Baseball*, an 18-hour history of our national pastime, provides a look at American society through a sport full of tradition and lore.

BUSH, GEORGE H.W.: 16,23

The father of President George W.

Bush and Florida Governor John ("Jeb") Bush, **George H.W. Bush** was elected 41st president in 1988 after serving two terms as vice president under Ronald Reagan. He was defeated in a bid for re-election by Bill Clinton. Bush enlisted in the U.S. Navy on his 18th birthday and became its youngest pilot when he earned his wings. He flew 58 combat missions during World War II and was awarded the Distinguished Flying Cross for bravery after his plane was shot down in action over water. A graduate of Yale University, Bush began his political career in 1967 with his election to Congress from Texas. He later was ambassador to the United Nations and director of the Central Intelligence Agency.

BUSH, GEORGE W.: 34

After serving six years as governor of Texas, **George W. Bush** won his first term in 2000 in a historically close election over Vice President Al Gore. He won re-election in 2004 over Massachusetts Senator John Kerry. Prior to his governorship, he was managing general partner of the Texas Rangers baseball club. He is a graduate of Yale University and served in the Air National Guard as a fighter pilot.

BUTTONS, RED: 41

A composer, author, actor, and comedian, **Red Buttons** began his entertainment career singing on street corners before moving on to telling jokes in New York's Catskill Mountains resorts. Born Aaron Chwatt in New York City's Lower East Side, his professional name resulted from a singing-waiting gig at New York City's Dinty Moore's Tavern, where his uniform featured 48 buttons to contrast with his red hair. In the 1940s, Buttons appeared on Broadway in *Vicki* and *Winged Victory* before landing his own television gig, *The Red Buttons Show*, on CBS in 1952, which won him an Emmy. His next big break came in 1957 with his Oscar-winning performance in *Sayonara* opposite Marlon Brando. Golden Globe nominations later followed for *Harlow* (1965) and *They Shoot Horses, Don't They?* (1969). To many of his younger fans, Buttons will be remembered as the ship employee in the 1972 disaster flick, *The Poseidon Adventure*. A TV regular on shows such as ABC's *The Love Boat* and *Knots Landing*, Buttons was also often featured on Dean Martin's televised celebrity roasts.

CAESAR, SID: 65

Legions of Americans would stay home on Saturday nights between 1950 and 1954 so they would not miss **Sid Caesar's** *Your Show of Shows* , a weekly series of comedy sketches that featured monologues by Caesar and sketches with him and comedienne Imogene Coca. Caesar, who displayed great range in both physical and vocal comedy, was skilled at mime, dialects, and foreign-language doubletalk. His show featured some of the best writers of the time—Mel Brooks, Carl Reiner, Larry Gelbart, Neil Simon, and Woody Allen, to name a few. From 1954 to 1957, he hosted *Caesar's Hour* and in 1958 was featured on the short-lived *Sid Caesar Invites You*. He returned to television in 1962 with *As Caesar Sees It*. He also appeared in numerous movies, most notably 1963's classic comedy, *It's a Mad, Mad, Mad, Mad World*, and was nominated for a Tony Award for his performance on Broadway in 1963's *Little Me*. A talented saxophonist who studied at the Juilliard School of Music, he performed in the orchestras of Charlie Spivak, Shep Fields, and Claude Thornhill before becoming an actor.

CAPPELLETTI, JOHN: 98

Penn State running back **John Cappelletti** may be remembered more for his acceptance speech at the 1973 Heisman Trophy banquet than for his outstanding play on the football field. In his speech, he credited his dying younger brother, Joey, with providing the inspiration for his accomplishments and presented Joey with

his trophy. John's tribute to his brother served as the basis of a touching television movie, *Something for Joey*. At Penn State, Cappelletti rushed for 1,117 yards as a junior in 1972, then topped it in 1973 with a 1,522-yard season that earned him the trophy. Cappelletti was drafted in the first round by the Los Angeles Rams in 1974 and retired in 1983 from the San Diego Chargers. In his eight professional seasons, Cappelletti rushed 824 times for 2,751 yards (a 3.3-yard average), and 24 touchdowns. He caught 135 passes for 1,233 yards and four touchdowns.

CARTER, GARY: 85, 94

As catcher for the New York Mets, **Gary Carter** became indelibly etched in baseball lore for igniting the team's 1986 World Series Game 6 comeback win against the Boston Red Sox with a clutch two-out single in the bottom of the 10th inning. The Mets went on to win the World Series. Carter's baseball career included four seasons with at least 100 runs batted in, as well as nine seasons in which he hit 20 or more home runs. He was named to 11 All-Star squads and won three Gold Glove awards. He was accepted into the Baseball Hall of Fame in 2003. Carter passed up dozens of football scholarship offers to join the Montreal Expos, where he played from 1974 through 1984. In 1978, he set a major league record by allowing just one passed ball in 157 games. Carter, who hit two home runs, was selected most valuable player of the 1981 All-Star Game. He finished his career with 2,092 hits and 324 home runs. He now runs The Gary Carter Foundation, which raises funds for various charities.

CASHMAN, TERRY: 38, 48

A former minor league baseball player in the Detroit Tigers organization, **Terry Cashman** always had great timing. His popular song, "Talkin' Baseball (Willie, Mickey, and 'The Duke')," which pays homage to the players of the 1950s, became a hit in 1981 when major league players went on strike. Since then, he has written and recorded dozens of baseball songs, including "The Money Doesn't Matter To Me," "Ichiro," "The Ballad of Herb Score," and versions of "Talkin' Baseball" for almost every Major League team. A more recent release is "A Tattered Flag in the Breeze" ("Michael's Song"), about the emotional September 21, 2001 game at Shea Stadium, the first played in New York after the terrorist attacks of September 11. Cashman appeared with his band, the Chevrons, on *American Bandstand* in the late 1950s and wrote several pop hits in the 60s. He and partner Tommy West produced singer/songwriter Jim Croce's early 1970s successes.

CLARK, DICK: 66

Known as the World's Oldest Teenager, **Dick Clark** showcased rock 'n' roll in America's homes via television. An ageless wonder who was born in 1929, Clark was a Philadelphia hit with *Bandstand* (1952) before ABC picked up the music and dance show in 1957. Clark changed the show's name to *American Bandstand* and ended the all-white performers policy by featuring such acts as Frankie Lymon and the Teenagers. By 1959, *American Bandstand* was reaching 20 million teenagers. NBC's series, *American Dreams*, has used Clark's *American Bandstand* as a cornerstone of the story line. In 1957, he founded Dick Clark Productions, which produced the *$10,000 Pyramid* game show, the *American Music Awards*, TV *Bloopers and Practical Jokes*, the Golden Globe Awards, and a perennial holiday favorite, *Dick Clark's Rockin' New Year's Eve*. Clark acted in *Spy Kids* (2001) and appears as himself in *Confessions of A Dangerous Mind* (2002). At the end of 2004, Clark proved to be mortal, suffering a stroke that forced him to miss hosting his New Year's Eve countdown from Times Square for the first time in 32 years.

CLINTON, BILL: 16, 22

A saxophone player who once toyed with becoming a professional musician, **Bill Clinton** became inspired to enter public service when he met President John F. Kennedy while serving as a delegate to Boys Nation. He won election to the presidency in 1992 and was re-elected in 1996. A graduate of Georgetown University and Yale Law School and a Rhodes Scholar at Oxford University, Clinton became governor of Arkansas in 1978. He lost a bid for a second term, then recaptured the governorship four years later. Quick with a smile and warm words, Clinton remains popular as a former president, international goodwill ambassador, and Democratic political strategist.

CONWAY, TIM: 57, 75

A funny man with a straight face, **Tim Conway** specialized in getting laughter from cast and audience on the 1970s hit, *The Carol Burnett Show*. Born Thomas Conway, the graduate of Bowling Green State University was discovered by comedienne Rose Marie of *The Dick Van Dyke Show*, who helped land him a spot on *The New Steve Allen Show*. The short, balding actor used his stature to gain laughs, first earning comedy wings with the 1960s sitcom *McHale's Navy*. *The Carol Burnett Show* helped Conway land roles in the Disney films, *The World's Greatest Athlete* (1973), *The Apple Dumpling Gang* (1975), *Gus* (1976), and *The Apple Dumpling Gang Rides Again*. A three-time Emmy

Award winner, Conway remerged during the 1980s with his comedic dwarf, Dorf, in a series of programs.

COSTAS, BOB: 73

Syracuse University graduate **Bob Costas** got his break covering the St. Louis American Basketball Association team for his hometown radio station, KMOX, in 1974. Thirty years later, Costas had garnered three Emmys and four national Sportscaster of the Year awards. From NBC's *Game Of the Week* baseball coverage to the network's *NFL Live* pre-game show (1984-1992), Costas has been an integral part of NBC sports coverage. Super Bowls, World Series, Winter Olympics, Summer Olympics, and NBA games highlight Costas' resume. He also hosted an NBC talk show, *Later, with Bob Costas*, from 1988 to 1994 and is the best-selling author of *Fair Ball: A Fan's Case for Baseball*. Since 2001, he has had a sports talk show on HBO.

COUSY, BOB: 114

Dubbed the "Houdini of the Hardwood" by sports writers, **Bob Cousy** brought razzle-dazzle to the National Basketball Association with amazing ball-handling skills and deft passes. Following an All-American career at Holy Cross, Cousy bounced to the Boston Celtics after his name was drawn out of the Chicago Stags dispersal draft. He arrived with Coach

Arnold "Red" Auerbach, who handed the 6-foot-1 Cousy the reins to an up-tempo game that allowed a dynasty to begin. Cousy led the league in assists for eight consecutive seasons (1953-60) and led the team to six consecutive NBA titles after fellow Hall of Famer Bill Russell joined the squad in 1956. Cousy played in 13 straight NBA All-Star games (MVP 1954, 1957) and finished his career with 16,960 points. Cousy later coached the Boston College Eagles (1963-1969) to a 117-38 record and finished coaching with the NBA's Cincinnati/Kansas City Royals (1969-1974). From 1974 to 1979, Cousy served as commissioner of the American Soccer League. He was elected in 1996 to the NBA's 50th Anniversary All-Time Team. The New York City-born Cousy was elected to the Basketball Hall of Fame in 1971.

COWANS, DAVE: 114

Dave Cowens did not play basketball until his high school junior year, but earned a full scholarship to play basketball at Florida State University. After averaging 19 points and 17 rebounds per game in college, the 6-foot-9 Cowens was taken with the fourth pick by the Boston Celtics in 1970. Critics said Cowens was too small to play center in the NBA, but he captured co-Rookie of the Year in 1971, averaging 17 points and 15 rebounds

per game. A member of the Celtics 1974 and 1976 NBA title teams, Cowens captured the 1973 League Most Valuable Player award (20.5 points and 16.2 rebounds per game). With a career average of 17.6 points and 13.6 rebounds per game, Hall of Fame honoree Cowens was named in 1996 to the NBA's 50th Anniversary All-Time Team. Cowens, who briefly served as Celtics player/coach in 1978-79, directed the Charlotte Hornets to the playoffs and later coached the Golden State Warriors.

CRAIG, JIM: 120, 123

With his timely saves, goalie **Jim Craig** was the backbone of the seventh-seeded U.S. hockey team that won an improbable gold medal in the 1980 Winter Olympics at Lake Placid. In the medal round against the Soviet Union, Craig kept the U.S. close as the Americans trailed 3-2 going into the final period. When Captain Mike Eruzione put the U.S. ahead, 4-3 with 10 minutes remaining, Craig took center stage, deflecting shot after shot until the miracle was complete. A 4-2 win over Finland secured the gold medal. Six nights after his team captured the gold, Craig started in the net for the National Hockey League's Atlanta Flames. He stopped 24 of the 25 shots he faced, leading the Flames to a 4-1 victory before a sellout crowd in Atlanta. It would prove to be the highlight of a star-crossed NHL career that never lived up to its potential. But Craig's place in sports history was secured in the 1980 games.

CRONKITE, WALTER: 56

For two decades, from 1961 to 1981, **Walter Cronkite** delivered America the nightly news for CBS and was considered the dean of television's anchormen. Cronkite started as a cub reporter for the *Kansas City Times* in 1937. In 1951, he and his CBS news associates created the format of reporting the news from headlines of the day as well as human-interest vignettes. An avid sailor, Cronkite named one of his boats "Assignment," purportedly so his secretary could tell callers truthfully that Walter was on Assignment and could not be reached. As a boy, Cronkite attended both the Republican and Democratic presidential conventions of 1928. Identified with television news in the 1960s and 1970s, Cronkite has appeared as himself, courtesy of videotape, in numerous films and television shows.

CROSBY, NORM: 39

Known as the Master of the Malapropism, **Norm Crosby** gained great fame murdering the English language on stage, on television, and in commercials. While serving in the U.S. Coast Guard on anti-submarine patrol, the Boston-area native lost part of his hearing due to concussions caused by depth charges. Crosby is well known as a co-host on Jerry Lewis's annual Labor Day telethon for the Muscular Dystrophy Association. Besides comedy, his other loves are charity work and golf.

DAVIS, JIM: 42, 46

In the 1980s, artist **Jim Davis'** "Garfield" ruled the comic-merchandising world. The Indiana native and Ball State University alumnus' fat, lazy, cynical cat could be found on everything from greeting cards to automobiles. The cartoonist came up with the idea for his cartoon after noting that the comic pages were filled with dogs and devoid of cats. Having grown up on a farm, Davis had plenty of experience with felines to draw upon. "Garfield" was born on June 19, 1978, debuting in 41 newspapers. Davis named the cat after his grandfather, James Garfield Davis. "Garfield" now runs in 2,570 newspapers with 263 million readers around the world. *The Guinness Book of World Records* even recognized "Garfield" as "The Most Widely Syndicated Comic Strip in the World." Davis' honors include four Emmy awards for outstanding animated program and the National Cartoonist Society award for best humor strip (1981 and 1985).

DAWSON, ANDRE: 83

Andre Dawson played 21 seasons for four teams, finishing with a .279 lifetime batting average, 438 home runs and 1,591 runs batted in. He captured the National League Rookie of the Year Award with the Montreal Expos in 1977. In 1987, as a Chicago Cub, Dawson won the National League Most Valuable Player Award. He was the first player to win it while playing for a last-place team. Drafted out of Florida A&M University by the Expos, the 6-foot-3 Dawson became a full-time major leaguer September 11, 1976. He starred in the Montreal Expos' vaunted outfield with Ellis Valentine and Tim Raines in the early 1980s, finishing second in the National League MVP race in 1981 and 1982. Thirteen times the eight-time All-Star outfielder surpassed 20 home runs in a season. The fleet-footed Dawson, who was later hobbled by knee injuries, stole 314 bases and twice hit two home runs in the same inning.

DELANEY, KIM: 55

An Emmy Award-winning actress on the ABC hit show, *NYPD Blue*, **Kim Delaney** began her career as a teen model. After studying acting with Bill Esper, the Philadelphia-born and - raised Delaney broke into television as Jenny Gardner on the soap opera *All My Children*. Her four-show guest appearance on *L.A. Law* in the late 1980s forecast a career in law and police shows. Delaney also appeared in the films *Rules of Engagement* and *Mission to Mars*. She became exposed to a new generation in the spring of 2005, playing Rebecca Bloom on the Fox show, *The O.C.* She also starred in television's *CSI: Miami* and *Philly*.

DELUISE, DOM: 43

Dom DeLuise has often been cast with actors Burt Reynolds, Mel Brooks, Gene Wilder, and Sid Caesar and actress Madeline Kahn. He has appeared in Brooks' classic films, *Blazing Saddles* (1974), *Silent Movie* (1976), *History of the World Part I* (1981), and *Robin Hood: Men in Tights* (1993). He is also the author of children's books and Italian cookbooks. His one starring film role came in the 1980 picture, *Fatso*. He was director of the 1979 film, *Hot Stuff*, and appeared in it with his wife, Carol, and sons Peter, Michael, and David. The family also appeared together in the television movie *Happy*. He was the comic relief as Captain Chaos in *Cannonball Run* (1980).

DILLER, PHYLLIS: 72

Phyllis Diller became one of the first major female stand-up acts in 1955 with her debut at San Francisco's famous Purple Onion. Diller's act featured a fictional husband, "Fang," which helped give her marital jokes real teeth. She poked fun at her looks with ease: "I was in a beauty contest once. I not only came in last, I was hit in the mouth by Miss Congeniality." Many of her tragedy-revisited jokes were followed by her unique laugh, which served as verbal punctuation. She had a part as Texas Guinan in the 1961 film, *Splendor in the Grass*, but found much of her fame on talk, variety, and game shows in the 1960s and 1970s. An accomplished pianist, Diller has performed with more than 100 symphony orchestras. Diller did voice-over work as the Queen in the 1998 Disney hit film, *A Bug's Life*. She retired from stand-up comedy in 2002 at the age of 84.

DIMAGGIO, DOM: 83, 92

Known as "The Little Professor" for his small (5-foot-9) stature and wire-rimmed glasses, **Dom DiMaggio** starred for the Boston Red Sox from 1940 to 1953. The younger brother of New York Yankees star Joe DiMaggio and journeyman ballplayer Vince DiMaggio, he amassed a lifetime batting average of .298 (four times batting .300 or better) and 1,680 hits in just 11 seasons. He missed three years of baseball (1943-1945) while serving in World War II. DiMaggio became a hero to undersized and nearsighted kids in New England, teaming with Ted Williams, Johnny Pesky, and Bobby Doerr to complete a formidable lineup that annually battled the mighty New York Yankees for the American League title.

DOERR, BOBBY: 88

Featured along with fellow letter writer Dom DiMaggio in author David Halberstam's book *The Teammates*, **Bobby Doerr** was the heart of the Boston Red Sox during much of the 1940s. Legendary hitter and Hall of Fame teammate Ted Williams said Doerr was the "silent captain" of those competitive Bosox teams. With a life-time batting average of .288, including a robust .409 in the 1946 World Series loss, Doerr was elected to the Baseball Hall of Fame in 1986. The Red Sox second baseman drove in more than 100 runs in six of his 14 seasons, with a career high of 120 in 1950 when teams played only 154 games. The slick fielder also held the American League record at one time by fielding 414 baseballs without an error and was considered one of the best double-play pivot men to ever play the position.

DONOVAN, ART: 98

Defensive tackle **Art Donovan** began his professional football career in 1950 with the Baltimore Colts, moving with the team to New York (Yankees) and Dallas (Texans), before returning to Baltimore for good in 1953. During his 12 National Football League seasons, Donovan was All-Pro five times and starred on the Colts' memorable 1958 and 1959 world championship teams. The Colts retired his number, 70, when he retired from football in 1962. In 1968, Donovan became the first Colt elected to the Pro Football Hall of Fame. His autobiography, Fatso, so named because he often arrived at training camp weighing more than 300 pounds, was published in 1987. Known for his joviality and good humor, the Boston College graduate and former U.S. Marine was a frequent late-night guest on Johnny Carson's and David Letterman's talk shows. He can be seen in the Bruce Willis movie, The *First Boy Scout*. Donovan owns and manages a country club near Baltimore.

DOWNS, HUGH: 49

Hugh Downs' television career is one for the record books. In 1985, The Guinness Book of World Records recognized Downs as having clocked more hours on television (10,347 at the time) than any other individual person. Starting as the announcer on *Kukla, Fran and Ollie* in 1949, Downs would go on to add a few of televisions greatest shows to his impressive resume. He was the announcer on Sid Caesar's Hour (1956-57), became the first talk show sidekick as the announcer of *The Jack Paar Show* (aka *The Tonight Show*, 1957-1962), emceed the classic game show *Concentration* (1958-1968), hosted NBC's *The Today Show* (1962-

1972) and co-anchored ABC's news-magazine show 20/20. Author of eight books, including *Thirty Dirty Lies About Old Age*, Downs has even dabbled in composing orchestral pieces and is an avid sailor as well as pilot despite being colorblind.

DUVALL, ROBERT: 61

Nominated six times for Academy Awards and winning once, **Robert Duvall** was once named the most versatile actor in the world by The Guinness Book of World Records. Although Duvall's big film break came playing Boo Radley in *To Kill a Mockingbird* in 1962, it was his 1972 performance as Tom Hagen in *The Godfather* that put Duvall on a par with acting's elite. A former New York City roommate of actors Dustin Hoffman and Gene Hackman, Duvall has many more film credits to remember, including Frank Hackett in *Network*; the surf-loving Colonel Kilgore in *Apocalypse Now*, Bull Meechum in *The Great Santini*, Mac Sledge in *Tender Mercies*, Max Mercy in *The Natural*, and Sonny Dewey in *The Apostle*. Also memorable are his work as Ned Pepper in *True Grit* and as the original Frank Burns in the 1970 movie *M*A*S*H*. A direct descendant of Civil War General Robert E. Lee, Duvall can trace his family tree back to President George Washington.

EBSEN, BUDDY: 66

A talented artist, **Buddy Ebsen** helped make the early 1960s television comedy, *The Beverly Hillbillies*, a runaway success as patriarch Jed Clampett. Ebsen had bounced around Hollywood's film and television stages prior to *Hillbillies*, nearly landing the role of the Tin Man in *The Wizard of Oz* before aluminum dust inhalation produced a violent illness that forced him to relinquish the role to Jack Haley. Ebsen later scored a TV drama success with *Barnaby Jones* in the early 1970s. The father of seven children, Ebsen was also a successful sailor, capturing racing trophies and owning a boat construction company.

ENBERG, DICK: 49

A member of the National Sportscasters and Sportswriters Hall of Fame, **Dick Enberg** began broadcasting sports in 1965 in Los Angeles as the voice of the California Angels baseball team, UCLA basketball team, and the Los Angeles Rams football team. He joined NBC sports in 1975 and over the next 25 years covered professional football, baseball, basketball, golf, and horse racing. A graduate of Central Michigan University and Indiana University, where he earned master's and doctorate degrees, Enberg entered broadcasting after working as an assistant professor and assistant baseball coach at California State University, Northridge

(1961-1965). The 13-time Emmy winner became the fourth sportscaster to have a star on the Hollywood Walk of Fame. He switched to CBS in 2000, and now calls that network's professional football and college basketball action and the U.S. Open tennis tournament. He contributes to coverage of the Masters and PGA golf tournements.

ERSKINE, CARL: 82

Brooklyn Dodgers ace **Carl Erskine** pitched 12 seasons (1948-1960) for "Da Bums." Erskine compiled a lifetime record of 122-78 (2-2 in World Series) playing alongside legendary teammates Jackie Robinson, Roy Campanella, Duke Snider, and Gil Hodges. In 1950, Erskine led the National League in victories with 20. But it was his team leadership that made him such a valuable part of the Dodgers, where he served as player representative for eight seasons. A U.S. Navy veteran, Erskine coached Anderson University in his native Anderson, Indiana, for 12 seasons and his teams won four championships. To commemorate citizenship and his career as a Dodger, a bronze statue of Erskine has been placed in front of the Carl D. Erskine Rehabilitation and Sports Medicine Center in Anderson. The exploits of Erskine and his fellow Dodgers in the mid-1950s were captured in the book *The Boys of Summer* by author Roger Kahn.

ERUZIONE, MIKE: 120

A flick of the wrist against the vaunted Soviet Union defense changed a game, a nation, and **Mike Eruzione's** life forever. Team captain Eruzione's goal sealed the scrappy U.S. ice hockey team's upset win over the heavily favored Soviet hockey machine in the 1980 Winter Olympics at Lake Placid. The victory moved the team to the gold-medal game, which it won over Finland. Just weeks earlier, Eruzione and his teammates had been humiliated by the Russians in Madison Square Garden, losing 10-3. After an all-American career at Boston University, Eruzione played for two years with the Toledo Goaldiggers of the International Hockey League and won the McKenzie Award, which is presented annually to the most outstanding American-born hockey player in the league. After the Olympics, he never played competitive hockey again, working instead as a hockey broadcaster, motivational speaker, and director of development for Boston University's Athletic Department. He has been inducted into the Olympic Hall of Fame.

FOSSETT, STEVE: 19

If there is a land, air, or water record, **Steve Fossett** is interested in breaking it. On March 3, 2005, the millionaire adventurer became the first person to fly around the world solo without stopping or refueling. He did it in a custom-built plane that circled the globe in 67 hours, starting from Salina, Kansas. The investment banker had previously become the first person to circumnavigate the world alone in an unmotorized balloon, his journey lasting 14 days, 19 hours in July 2002. It was on his sixth attempt that Fossett established the record, one of 10 air records he has set. Fossett has also circumnavigated the earth as a sailor and, since 1993, has set 21 official world records in sailing, including sailing across the Atlantic Ocean in four days, 17 hours (October 2001), besting the previous mark by 43 hours, 35 minutes. In his free time, Fossett has swum the English Channel, participated in the Ironman Triathlon and the Iditarod dogsled race, and burned rubber in the 24-hour automobile race at Le Mans, France.

GAGLIARDI, JOHN: 102

A little-known sports story is the amazing success of Saint John's University football coach **John Gagliardi**, who has paced the Collegeville, Minnesota, sidelines for the past 52 years. On November 8, 2003, Gagliardi became the all-time winningest college football coach as his Johnnies' victory moved him past the legendary Grambling head coach Eddie Robinson. Gagliardi, who will begin his 57th coaching season in 2005, has 421 wins (a 421-117-11 record), 397 of them at St. John's and 24 during four seasons at Carroll

College in Helena, Montana. Since he took the St. John's job in 1953, Gagliardi has coached the Division III Johnnies to four national championships, 37 consecutive winning seasons, and 26 conference titles. His 1993 team averaged 61.5 points per game to establish a national record. The subject of author Austin Murphy's book, *Sweet Season* (2001), Gagliardi has defied time (he'll be 79 in November 2005) and confounded critics with a unique coaching philosophy that forbids blocking sleds or dummies, scholarships, spring practices, mandatory weight lifting, whistles, pads and tackling in practice, and the title of "Coach" (he insists on being called John). He confines practice sessions to 90 minutes or less.

GELBART, LARRY: 77

After writing gags for radio programs such as The Danny Thomas Show while still in high school, **Larry Gelbart** quickly climbed the comedy writers' ladder. He hooked up with Sid Caesar's Your Show of Shows in 1953 and became a success on Caesar's Hour. Teaming with Carl Reiner, Neil Simon, and Mel Brooks, Gelbart won two Emmys for his comedy work. He crossed over to theater in the early 1960s, co-creating the Broadway musical smash, *A Funny Thing Happened on the Way to the Forum*, starring Zero Mostel. With *Forum*, Gelbart won the first of his three Tony Awards. After nine years living in London, Gelbart returned to television, producing and writing 97 segments of *M*A*S*H*. Completing his triple-threat résumé, Gelbart wrote the screenplays for two hit films, *Oh, God!*, starring George Burns and John Denver in 1977, and *Tootsie*, Dustin Hoffman's 1982 blockbuster. *Tootsie* earned Gelbart an Academy Award nomination as well as best screenplay awards from the New York, Los Angeles, and National Film Critic societies.

GRIFFIN, ARCHIE: 91,106

The only two-time Heisman Trophy winner (1974 and 1975), running back **Archie Griffin** may see his accomplishment stand for a long time as today's college players often turn professional before completing school. Described by Ohio State University coach Woody Hayes as the greatest player he ever coached, Griffin rushed for a total of 5,589 yards, which still stands as an OSU record. He also scored 26 touchdowns, with a record 6.13 yards-per-carry average. His record of 34 career 100-yard games and his string of 31 straight regular season games of 100 yards or more still stands. The accomplishments didn't just come on the field. After his senior year, Archie won the National Collegiate Athletic Association's Top Five Award, which honors performance in academics, athletics, and leadership—the highest award that the NCAA presents. Griffin has been inducted into the College Football Hall of Fame as well as the National High School Hall of Fame. He spent eight years with the Cincinnati Bengals after being drafted in the first round. He now works at Ohio State as associate athletic director.

GROAT, DICK: 85

A two-sport star at Duke University, **Dick Groat** elected baseball as a full-time profession despite achieving All-American status in basketball for the Blue Devils. Groat began his 14-season career on June 19, 1952 with the Pittsburgh Pirates and finished with a lifetime batting average of .286. In 1960, Groat helped lead the National League Pirates to a shocking World Series victory over the vaunted New York Yankees in seven games. Groat batted better than .300 four times, with a career-best season in 1963 for the St. Louis Cardinals (.319 average, 201 hits, six home runs, 73 runs batted in).

HACKETT, BUDDY: 69, 74

Born Leonard Hacker in Brooklyn in 1924, the late **Buddy Hackett** cut his sharp comic teeth in New York's Catskill Mountain resorts, joining such luminaries as Milton Berle, Henny Youngman, and Red Buttons. Hackett's rubbery face and stilted speech pattern found their home on the stages of Las Vegas and Atlantic City, where his salty act never lost its flavor. Hackett's two biggest commercial movie hits came as the sideman next to Robert Preston in 1962's *The Music Man* and in the star-studded Stanley Kramer 1963 film, *It's a Mad, Mad, Mad, Mad World*. He also appeared in the 1999 Fox series, *Action*, playing chauffeur/uncle to star Jay Mohr's movie-mogul character.

HALL, MONTY: 54

The Canadian-born and -raised **Monty Hall** co-created *Let's Make A Deal* (1963-1986), a TV hit that combined the best of Halloween-costumed audience members with impulse shopping. He presided over the wackiness with aplomb and razor-sharp wit. In 1988, Canada bestowed its highest honor on Hall, awarding him the prestigious Order of Canada for his humanitarian works in his native country and around the world. Hall is the father of Tony Award-winning actress Joanna Gleason, television writer/director Sharon Hall, and Emmy Award-winning television producer Richard Hall.

HAMLISCH, MARVIN: 46

Pianist/composer **Marvin Hamlisch** was on his way to greatness when, at the age of seven, he became the youngest performer ever accepted by the prestigious Juilliard School of Music. In 1976, Hamlisch won the Pulitzer Prize and a Tony Award for the Broadway hit musical, *A Chorus Line*. In 1973, he became the first individual to win three Academy Awards in one night, sweeping all three music categories. Hamlisch collected Oscars for the best song, "The Way We Were," in the movie of the same name, and for the movie's score. His third award was for adapting Scott Joplin's ragtime music to *The Sting*. He has also collected four Grammys, four Emmys, and three Golden Globe awards. In a rare film appearance, Hamlisch plays himself in the comedy *How to Lose A Guy In 10 Days*.

HARWELL, ERNIE: 36, 38

The voice of Detroit Tigers baseball for 42 years, **Ernie Harwell** made his major league debut in 1948 as the only radio broadcaster to be part of a trade. Atlanta Crackers President Earl Mann agreed to release Harwell to Brooklyn if the Dodgers' Branch Rickey would send Montreal minor league catcher Cliff Dapper to Atlanta to manage. Brief stops as the New York Giants' and Baltimore Orioles' play-by-play announcer preceded his move to the Motor City in 1960. Harwell, a graduate of Emory University, was part of history as he called New York Giant Bobby Thomson's famous playoff home run in 1951 during the first coast-to-coast telecast of a major sporting event. He was the 1981 recipient of the Baseball Hall of Fame Ford C. Frick Award.

HOWARD, FRANK: 94

A larger-than-life figure, the 6-foot-7, 255-pound **Frank Howard** dominated the plate from 1958 to 1973 with tape-measure home runs that have produced tall tales about the distance the ball traveled. Known as "Hondo" by teammates and "Capital Punishment" by opposing pitchers, Howard began his 16-season career as a Los Angeles Dodger in 1958 and had brief playing time in 1958 and 1959 before winning rookie-of-the-year honors in 1960 with a .268 batting average, 23 home runs, and 77 runs batted in. Howard, whose best season with Los Angeles came in 1962 (.296 average, 31 HR, 119 RBI), was dealt from the National League penthouse to the American League cellar when the Washington Senators acquired the big first baseman in 1965. From 1967 to 1970, Howard hit 36, 44, 48, and 44 home runs, respectively, in an era when pitchers dominated hitters.

HOWARD, KEN: 36

For all his acting accomplishments, **Ken Howard** will forever be known to legions of sports junkies as Coach Ken Reeves in the CBS hit *The White Shadow* (1978-1981). The 6-foot-7

Howard co-created the show based partly on his experience as the only white player on his high school basketball team. The Emmy Award-winning Howard attended the Yale School of Drama before snagging a part in playwright Neil Simon's Broadway production of *Promises, Promises* in 1968. He starred as Thomas Jefferson in the Tony-winning musical *1776* and garnered a Tony Award for his performance in *Child's Play*. He costarred in the 1980s prime time shows *The Colbys* and *Dynasty*, and appears on Larry David's *Curb Your Enthusiasm*.

HULL, BRETT: 123

Very few sons of Hall of Fame athletes ever achieve or surpass their famous fathers' successes. **Brett Hull** is one who did. After he scored his 1,000th National Hockey League point, he and his legendary dad, Bobby Hull, became the only father-son combination to each score 1,000 points. Hull was the 117th player picked in the 1984 NHL draft. He wasted little time becoming a prolific goal scorer, lighting the lamp in his very first game. The hard-shooting winger spent 11 seasons in St. Louis, winning the Hart Trophy in 1991 when he scored 86 goals and amassed a total of 131 points. He was traded to the Dallas Stars in 1998 and the Stars won the Stanley Cup the following year. After three years with Dallas, he signed with the Detroit Red Wings and helped them win the Stanley Cup in 2002. He joined the Phoenix Coyotes in 2004.

IRVIN, MONTE: 88

Statistics do not tell the full story of **Monte Irvin's** great career because he spent five years with the Newark Eagles of the Negro Leagues and 68 games in the Mexican League prior to joining the New York Giants in 1949. A high-average hitter with power, the 6-foot-1, 195-pound Irvin teamed with the legendary Willie Mays to give the Giants a lethal 1-2 punch during his eight years with the team. Irvin, who was elected to the Baseball Hall of Fame in 1973, played a major role in the Giants' two pennant-winning seasons (1951 and 1954), batting .458 in the 1951 World Series and stealing home. A four-sport star at East Orange (New Jersey) High School, Irvin became a professional baseball player at the age of 17. It's estimated that he batted .350 during his five years in the Negro Leagues. He once posted a .397 average in winning the Mexican League's most valuable player award. A career .293 hitter, Irvin collected 731 hits in his major league career with his best season coming in 1951 (.312 average, 24 HR, 121 runs, 94 RBI).

IRWIN, HALE: 109

Hale Irwin's first Professional

Golfers' Association tour win came in 1971 at the Sea Pines Heritage Classic, four years after winning the National Collegiate Athletic Association championship as a University of Colorado student. In all, he won 20 PGA tournaments, including the U.S. Open in 1974, 1979, and 1990. The Missouri native has enjoyed even greater success on the Champions Tour (formerly the Senior PGA Tour), which he joined in 1995. As of June 2005, he had 42 titles and is the all-time money winner with more than $21 million in earnings.

JENKINS, FERGUSON: 81

Perhaps no pitcher in baseball history is more overlooked and underappreciated than **Ferguson Jenkins**, who toiled at the height of his career for the hapless Chicago Cubs. For six consecutive seasons, Jenkins racked up 20 or more victories. The hard-throwing, 6-foot-5, 200-pound right-hander joined the Cubs in 1966 to begin a remarkable stretch capped in 1971 with a 24-13 record, a 2.77 earned-run average, 30 complete games, and the National League Cy Young Award. Traded to the Texas Rangers in 1973, Jenkins would go on in 1974 to win a career-high 25 games. He won 20 or more games seven times. Jenkins' lifetime record, 284-226, with a 3.34 ERA, is particularly impressive because his teams never made a single post-season appearance.

Jenkins was enshrined in the Baseball Hall of Fame in 1991.

JENNER, BRUCE: 123

Bruce Jenner's record-breaking gold medal victory in the Decathlon at the 1976 Summer Olympic Games in Montreal catapulted the New York native to a career as a motivational speaker, television personality, sports commentator, commercial spokesperson for nationally known companies, entrepreneur, actor, producer, and author. Jenner appeared in the 1980 film *Can't Stop The Music*, and starred in the NBC television movie, *Grambling's White Tiger*. He is the author of several books, including *Finding the Champion Within*, which is the theme of his motivational speeches. A winner of the Sullivan Award as the nation's top amateur athlete, Jenner was even the Eastern United States water skiing champion.

JONES, BERT: 97

Quarterback **Bert Jones** was drafted by the Baltimore Colts in 1973 after a college career at Louisiana State University. During his eight seasons with the team, the Colts won division titles in 1975, 1976, and 1977. His best year was 1976, when he threw for 3,104 yards and a career-high 24 touchdowns. The Associated Press named him the National Football League's most valuable player and offensive player of the year. He played four games for the Los Angeles Rams in 1982 before back injuries forced his retirement.

KEANE, BIL: 53

"The Family Circus," a timeless portrait of family life, was created by **Bil Keane** in 1960. Today, the famous circle of suburban family hijinks, inspired by his own children and grandchildren, is found in a record 1,500 newspapers around the world. If a daily dose of Billy, Dolly, and PJ is not enough, more than 60 published collections and three television specials are available. There are over 14 million "Family Circus" books in print. In 1983, Keane was named cartoonist of the year by the National Cartoonist Society.

KINER, RALPH: 83

In his 10-year career between 1946 and 1955, **Ralph Kiner** was one of baseball's premier sluggers. In each of his first seven seasons with the Pittsburgh Pirates, Kiner led the National League in home runs, twice hitting more than 50 per year. If not for a bad injury that forced him to retire at the age of 32, Kiner might have finished among the all-time slugging greats. In 1975, he was elected to the Baseball Hall of Fame. Later, generations of New York Mets fans knew Ralph Kiner as a baseball broadcaster with a knack for a classic quip.

KING, BEN E.: 69

Born Benjamin Earl Nelson in 1938, **Ben E. King** had his big break in 1958 when his doo-wop outfit, the Five Crowns, was re-dubbed the Drifters after lead vocalist Clyde MacPhatter departed. Working with the hit songwriting duo of Jerry Leiber and Mike Stoller, King made his first major mark singing lead on "There Goes My Baby," a song he co-wrote. In the next two years, King and the Drifters scored hits with "Dance With Me," "This Magic Moment," and "Save the Last Dance for Me." King quit the group in 1960 over a salary dispute, but found even bigger success as a solo artist. His "Spanish Harlem" was a Top 10 hit that was followed by his signature song, "Stand By Me." The latter song was featured in the 1986 Rob Reiner movie of the same name. King continues to record and tour all over the world.

KNIGHT, PHILIP H.: 29

Philip Knight's creation of Nike, the Oregon-based athletic shoe, clothing, and sporting goods behemoth, is a great example of turning a personal passion into a big success story. A former University of Oregon track star, Knight teamed with his former track coach, Bill Bowerman, to form Blue Ribbon Sports, Inc. in 1968. Bowerman made the first prototype running shoes using a waffle iron and Knight sold them out of the trunk of his car at track meets. In 1972, Knight renamed the company Nike, after the Greek goddess of victory. Under Knight's direction, which included the signing of college hoop star Michael Jordan and many other famous athletes to use Nike products, Nike became the world's largest shoe maker and a $12 billion business. The Nike swoosh is one of the most recognizable brand trademarks in the world.

KRZYZEWSKI, MIKE: 80, 117

Duke University men's basketball coach **Mike Krzyzewski** posts an impressive résumé: three National Collegiate Athletic Association titles (1991, 1992, and 2001), 12 national Coach of the Year honors, member of the Naismith Basketball Hall of Fame (2001), and best-selling author of two books on basketball. A three-year letterman at the U.S. Military Academy, Coach K learned from the legendary Bobby Knight at Army and later as Knight's graduate assistant coach at Indiana University. His work off the court with the Children's Miracle Network and the V Foundation, started by his dear friend and coaching rival, the late Jim Valvano, adds luster to his accomplishments on the court.

KUCHAR, MATT: 109

Matt Kuchar burst onto the national golf scene in 1998 as the top amateur at the Masters Tournament (21st overall) and U.S. Open (14th overall). At that point, he could have turned professional with endorsements worth millions of dollars, but Kuchar chose to remain an amateur and finish his final two years at Georgia Tech. Kuchar won the 1997 U.S. Amateur championship, succeeding Tiger Woods as the crown holder. A member of the 1999 Walker Cup team, Kuchar turned professional in 2001 and won the Honda Classic in 2002.

LAETTNER, CHRISTIAN: 116

Christian Laettner was a member of the United States Olympic Team that captured the gold medal at the 1992 Summer Games in Barcelona, Spain. But he is remembered at Duke University for what fans have called perhaps the greatest shot in college basketball history. In a memorable NCAA Tournament Regional Final against Kentucky in 1992, Laettner's Duke team was on the brink of losing an opportunity to defend its national title. But Laettner, the 1992 College Player of the Year, grabbed a three-quarter-court pass from Grant Hill, pivoted, and stroked a jump shot to win the game at the buzzer. Laettner and his Blue Devil teammates won NCAA titles in 1991 and 1992. Laettner was drafted by Minnesota with the third overall pick in 1992, and later made the Miami Heat his sixth professional team.

LARUSSA, TONY: 96

Anthony "Tony" LaRussa did not let a brief playing career (132 games in six seasons) deter his dream of a successful life in major-league baseball. LaRussa found his niche as a big league manager in 1979, when he began a nine-year stint with the Chicago White Sox. That was followed by ten years at the helm of the Oakland Athletics. Since 1995, he has been manager of the St. Louis Cardinals. He has guided all three teams into the baseball post-season. From 1988 to 1990, LaRussa's Oakland teams captured three consecutive American League pennants and a 1989 World Series sweep over the San Francisco Giants. In 2004, his Cardinals won the National League pennant. With more than 2,000 career wins, LaRussa is regarded by many baseball experts as one of the finest managers ever. He has received manager-of-the-year honors at each of his three big league stops. An animal activist, LaRussa helped create Tony LaRussa's Animal Rescue Foundation that helps find homes for dogs and cats.

LEONARD, ELMORE: 24, 33

Born in New Orleans, **Elmore Leonard** spent part of World War II in the U.S. Navy. He studied English literature at the University of Detroit before embarking on a career in advertising as a copywriter. His first pub-

lished work came in 1951 with the western, *Trail of the Apache*. His first novel to reach Hollywood was *Hombre*, featuring a young Paul Newman. His first crime novel, *The Big Bounce*, set him on his current Hollywood path, which includes *Out of Sight* (1998), featuring George Clooney and Jennifer Lopez, and 1995's *Get Shorty*, starring John Travolta.

LEONARD, SUGAR RAY: 119

Taking a page from Muhammad Ali's playbook, the brash **Ray Leonard** from Palmer Park, Maryland, landed in Ali trainer Angelo Dundee's corner after capturing the gold medal in the 1976 Summer Olympics in Montreal. Under Dundee's eye, Leonard won championships in five weight classes to become the first boxer to surpass $100 million in fight purses. In the 1980s, Leonard had classic duels with Roberto Duran, Thomas Hearns, and Marvin Hagler. His only loss in his first 35 professional fights came in his 1980 match against Duran, in which the light-footed, dancing Leonard set out to prove to the boxing world he could slug it out with the Fists of Stone. Leonard went the 15 rounds toe-to-toe with Duran, but lost a close decision. Named after legendary singer Ray Charles, Leonard adopted boxer Sugar Ray Robinson's style and moniker. Leonard, who was retired from 1984-1987, returned to the ring for a $12 million bout against World Boxing Council middleweight champion Hagler, winning a split decision. In 2005, as a fight promoter, he teamed with *Survivor* creator Mark Burnett to produce a boxing-reality show, *The Contender*, for NBC.

LEWIS, JERRY: 68

Now known primarily for his annual telethon to raise funds for the Muscular Dystrophy Association, **Jerry Lewis** became a comedic star playing off the suave Dean Martin. In 1946, when their nightclub act took off in Atlantic City, Lewis went from making $250 per week to $5,000. Over the next decade, the duo made 16 movies, hosted successful television and radio shows, and set nightclub engagement records. In 1977, Lewis was nominated for the Nobel Peace Prize for his MDA efforts. His screen credits include *The King of Comedy*, The *Bellboy*, *Cinderfella*, and *The Caddy*. The father of five, including recording artist Gary Lewis, he has fought constant pain and ills over the last decade as the result of a lung condition. But he has not let his woes stop his artistic passion or his fight against muscular dystrophy.

LINKLETTER, ART: 70

Art Linkletter became famous on the radio with shows that translated well to television in the 1950s. He was the host of *House Party*, which ran on CBS radio and television for 25 years, and *People are Funny*, which ran on NBC radio and TV for 19 years. He was best known for his interviews with children, which he called "Kids Say the Darndest Things." That segment spawned a bestselling book (number one for two years) and a television program of the same name. Born in Moose Jaw, Saskatchewan (Canada), Linkletter also had other shows on television—*Hollywood Talent Scouts*, *Life With Linkletter*, and *The Heart of Show Business*, as well as the movie, *Champagne for Caesar*, He is the author of 23 books, the most recent being *Old Age Is Not for Sissies*. Linkletter's love of children led him to work with the National Easter Seals Foundation, the National Heart Foundation, and Goodwill Industries. He is the national chairman of the United Seniors Association.

LOTT, RONNIE: 95

A first-round draft pick of the San Francisco 49ers in 1981 after an All-American career at the University of Southern California, defensive back **Ronnie Lott** immediately helped transform a cellar-dwelling team into a Super Bowl champion. He earned All-Pro honors as a rookie and started all 16 regular games and three post-season games in earning the first of his four Super Bowl rings. When Lott retired in 1994, after brief stops with the Los Angeles Raiders and New York Jets, he had amassed more than 1,000 tackles and 63 interceptions. In 1995, he was named to the NFL's 75th Anniversary Team. Lott, a 10-time Pro Bowl selection, was inducted into the Pro Football Hall of Fame in 2000.

LUJACK, JOHNNY: 98

Called by many college football experts the greatest T-formation quarterback ever, **Johnny Lujack** led the University of Notre Dame to three national titles (1943, 1946, and 1947) and captured the Heisman Trophy in 1947. Lujack also earned letters in basketball, baseball, and track while at Notre Dame. He was the Chicago Bears' first-round draft choice in 1948 and was named All-Pro as a defensive back. He took over as starting quarterback in 1949 and was an All-Pro again in 1950. As the Bears' quarterback in 1949, he set a National Football League record of six touchdown passes in one game in a 52-21 victory over the Chicago Cardinals. After retiring from the NFL in 1951, Lujack served two years as an assistant coach for Notre Dame. He was elected to the National Football Foundation and College Hall of Fame in 1960.

LYNN, FRED: 88

In 1975, Boston Red Sox center fielder **Fred Lynn** achieved the rare honor of being named both the American League's rookie of the year and its most valuable player. After attending college at the University of Southern California, where he helped guide the Trojans to three College World Series titles, Lynn catapulted to fame in leading the Bosox to the 1975 World Series. A four-time Gold Glove winner, Lynn's finest season may have been 1979 when he hit a league-leading .333, smashed 39 home runs, and drove in 122 runs. In the 1983 All-Star Game in Chicago, Lynn led the American League to victory by hitting the first All-Star grand slam. In 1985, Lynn was traded to the Baltimore Orioles, where he played for four years. He finished his career in 1990 with 306 home runs and a .283 lifetime batting average.

MACKEY, JOHN: 97, 105

Tight end **John Mackey**, a Number Two draft pick from Syracuse University, played nine seasons with the Baltimore Colts before finishing his career with the San Diego Chargers. A former NFL Players Association president, Mackey snagged 331 receptions and scored 38 touchdowns. Only the second tight end ever inducted into the Pro Football Hall of Fame (1992), he earned his reputation by making big plays. His reputation was underscored in 1966, when the All-Pro tight end produced six touchdown receptions of 50 or more yards.

MALDEN, KARL: 59

Former mill worker **Karl Malden** gambled on becoming an actor at the height of the Depression. Teaming up with famed director Elia Kazan, Malden soon starred on Broadway in Arthur Miller's *All My Sons* and Tennessee Williams' *A Streetcar Named Desire*. Later, he won a Best Supporting Actor Oscar for his performance as Mitch in the 1951 film version of *Streetcar*. He also starred in *On the Waterfront* (1954). He played U.S. Hockey Team coach Herb Brooks in the 1983 television movie *Miracle on Ice*. In 1985, Malden won an Emmy for *Fatal Vision*. He was president of the Academy of Motion Picture Arts and Sciences from 1988 to 1992 and published *When Do I Start?: A Memoir*. He also starred in the hit TV show, *The Streets of San Francisco* (1972-1977). Not bad for a Chicago lad who did not speak a word of English until kindergarten.

MANTEGNA, JOE: 70

One of the stars of the CBS hit, *Joan of Arcadia*, **Joe Mantegna** rose to fame and a Tony Award as Ricky Roma in playwright David Mamet's *Glengarry Glen Ross*. After critical success in *Compromising Positions* (1985), Mantegna played the slimy contractor Art Shirk in the 1986 Tom Hanks flick *The Money Pit*. His first high-profile role came as George Raft in the gangster picture *Bugsy* (1991). He is also

seen in lesser-known film gems such as *Homicide* (1991), *Queens Logic* (1991), *Searching for Bobby Fischer* (1993), and *Liberty Heights* (1999). The Chicago native's love of the Cubs can be found in his many performances of *Bleacher Bums*, which he wrote and starred in, and his voice-over work on the HBO baseball special, *When It Was a Game 2*.

MARTIN, DICK: 57

"You bet your bippy!" was actor/comedian **Dick Martin's** trademark line from Rowan & Martin's Laugh-In, the smash 1960s show he co-hosted with Dan Rowan. On television, Martin was always the life of the party, appearing on *The Dean Martin Summer Show*, *The Lucille Ball Show*, or *Match Game PM*. Few know Martin also directed many television shows, such as *In the Heat of the Night*, *Newhart*, *Family Ties*, and *The Bob Newhart Show*. Martin was even a regular passenger on ABC's *The Love Boat*, making five voyages.

MATHESON, TIM: 52

In his premier role, **Tim Matheson** starred as the smooth-talking, sex-obsessed Eric "Otter" Stratton in *National Lampoon's Animal House* with John Belushi (1978). Matheson was also cast as sleazy Alan Stanwyk, the straight man for comedian Chevy Chase in *Fletch*. Born in 1947,

Matheson had his break as the voice of Jonny Quest on the 1964 cartoon television series of the same name. Voiceover work and appearances on TV series constituted the bulk of Matheson's work until producer Ivan Reitman came calling with *Animal House*. Matheson now directs television shows, his work includes *Numb3rs*, *Cold Case*, *Ed*, *Third Watch*, and *Without a Trace*.

MATHIAS, BOB: 120

Born in Tulare, California, **Bob Mathias** suffered from anemia as a child and had to be put on a special diet. In 1948, at the age of 17, he became the youngest person to ever win the gold medal in the decathlon, at the Summer Olympics in London. Prior to that year, Mathias had never competed in the grueling, 10-event decathlon. Four years later, he became the first to win consecutive Olympic decathlons. Unbeaten in 11 decathlons in his career, he won four national Amateur Athletic Union championships and set three world records. Mathias, who won the Sullivan Award in 1948 as the nation's top amateur athlete, enrolled at Stanford University in 1949 and played two seasons of football for the Indians. In 1952, the 6-foot-3, 204-pounder became the only athlete to ever play in the Rose Bowl and compete in the Olympics in the same year. In 1961, he starred in *The Bob Mathias Story* on the silver screen. Elected to the U.S. House of Representatives in 1966, the Californian served four consecutive terms before becoming director of the U.S. Olympic Training Center in Colorado.

MCCAIN, JOHN: 17, 31

John McCain has served his country for nearly five decades. After graduating from the U.S. Naval Academy in 1958, he took to the sky as a naval aviator. After his plane was shot down in 1967, he was imprisoned in Hanoi for $5^1/_2$ years. In 1982, McCain was elected to Congress as a U.S. Representative from Arizona. Four years later, he replaced Arizona's legendary Barry Goldwater in the Senate. Charming, candid, and considered something of a maverick, McCain ran unsuccessfully for the Republican presidential nomination in 2000, but has remained influential on the national scene and is viewed as a possible presidential candidate in 2008.

MCKAY, JIM: 36

Jim McKay is probably best known to sports fans as the host of ABC's *Wide World of Sports* between 1961 and 1998. He is also remembered for his coverage of 12 Olympics, most notably the 1972 Summer Games in Munich when terrorists killed 11 members of the Israeli team. McKay has also covered a wide variety of special events, including the Kentucky Deby, the Indianapolis 500, and the British Open golf tournament. He has won numerous awards for journalism, including two Emmys and the George Polk Award for his sports and news coverage of the 1972 Olympics. In 1988, McKay was inducted into the U.S. Olympic Hall of Fame.

MICKELSON, PHIL: 108, 111, 124

In the history of golf, very few left-handers have made it into the ranks of the elite professionals. **Phil Mickelson**, winner of the 2004 Masters Tournament, is the best of that small group, which includes Canada's Mike Weir, Masters champion in 2003, and New Zealand's Bob Charles, who won the British Open in 1963. Mickelson, who is right-handed in everything else, learned to play the game mirroring his father's swing. A top U.S. amateur, he won his first PGA event while attending Arizona State University in 1991. Since joining the professional ranks, he has won more than 20 tournaments, but has always had trouble with the majors. That is what made Mickelson's comeback in 2004 on Augusta's fabled back nine so special. He sank a birdie putt on the 18th hole to seal the Masters victory. Mickelson is one of only three golfers to win the National Collegiate Athletic Association and

U.S. Amateur championships in the same year; the other two are Tiger Woods and Jack Nicklaus.

MILLER, MITCH: 45

Mitch Miller, an oboist, conductor, and record producer, began his career playing the oboe in symphonies and doing freelance work. His hard work and record company contacts finally landed him at Columbia Records in 1950, where he quickly moved from classical performances to scouting and producing. Miller signed 1950s stalwarts Doris Day, Tony Bennett, Ray Conniff, and Johnny Mathis. Miller's own "Yellow Rose of Texas" became his greatest hit single. From 1961 to 1966, Miller starred in NBC's *Sing Along With Mitch Miller*. The hit show featured Miller robustly conducting his orchestra as folksy singers belted out his favorite songs and the lyrics scrolled across the screen.

MOLITOR, PAUL: 81, 92

As a member of the Milwaukee Brewers, Minnesota Twins, and Toronto Blue Jays, **Paul Molitor** played 21 seasons, rapping out 3,319 base hits and producing a lifetime batting average of .306. He was voted to the All-Star Team seven times and inducted into the Baseball Hall of Fame in 2004. Molitor, who began at second base with the Milwaukee Brewers in 1978, may have added to his impressive offensive numbers had he not been sidelined with injuries for 500 games—equal to missing three seasons. A consistent line-drive hitter with quick bat speed, Molitor never hit more than 22 home runs in a season and his 1996 total of 113 runs batted in was a career high. But the man called "The Ignitor" finished in the top 10 in batting 11 times. Known for his speed early in his career, Molitor finished with 504 stolen bases and in 1987 produced a 39-game hitting streak. The 1993 World Series most valuable player for the champion Toronto Blue Jays (.500 average, two home runs, 10 runs scored), Molitor got better with age. In 1996, playing for the Minnesota Twins at age 40, he hit .341 with an American League-leading 225 hits and 113 runs batted in. Legendary hitter Ted Williams often said Molitor's sweet swing reminded him of Joe DiMaggio.

MOORE, LENNY: 99

Penn State standout **Lenny Moore** was the Baltimore Colts' Number One draft choice in 1956; he had an immediate impact on the franchise and was named rookie of the year. A combination flanker and tailback, Moore was a double-threat player who confounded National Football League defenses for a decade. On the way to Baltimore's first NFL title in 1958, Moore tallied 1,638 yards from scrimmage and 14 touchdowns in a 12-game season. That

year, he was named to the All-Pro team for the first of five times. The NFL's most valuable player in 1964, Moore scored touchdowns in 18 consecutive games from 1963 to 1965 and finished his Hall of Fame career with 113 touchdowns. He retired after the 1967 season and was enshrined in the Hall in 1975.

MORENO, RITA: 64

Singer and actress **Rita Moreno** has won an Oscar, a Tony, an Emmy, and a Grammy, the only woman to lay claim to the quadruple crown. Born Rosa Dolores Alverio in Puerto Rico, Moreno moved to New York with her mother as a young girl. By age 13, she had made her professional debut on Broadway as Angelina in *Skydrift*. By 19, Moreno had appeared in her first Hollywood film, *So Young, So Bad*. Her first big film break came in winning the role of the Asian Princess Tuptim in the film version of *The King and I*. In 1961, Moreno returned to Broadway as Anita in *West Side Story*. She played the same role in the film version and captured the Best Supporting Actress Academy Award. In 1971, Moreno was given a part in the PBS show, *The Electric Company*, for which she garnered a Grammy Award for the soundtrack. She won a Tony Award for her role on Broadway in *The Ritz* and Emmy awards for her television performances on *The Muppet Show* and

The Rockford Files. Moreno continues to perform on stage and in nightclubs all over the world.

NAVRATILOVA, MARTINA: 119, 122

One of the greatest female tennis players of all time, Czechoslovakia-born **Martina Navratilova** has won 58 Grand Slam events. She won Wimbledon singles titles a record nine times, with six straight from 1982 to 1987. Her on-court rivalry with Chris Evert (43-37 record) propelled women's tennis to new heights of popularity. Navratilova and partner Pam Shriver captured every Grand Slam doubles event in 1984. She also won three Australian Opens (1981, 1983, and 1985), two French Opens (1982 and 1984), and four U.S. Open singles titles (1983, 1984, 1986, and 1987). In 1986, Navratilova was Associated Press Female Athlete of the Year for the second time.

NELSON, BYRON: 112, 115

Known affectionately as "Lord Byron" by his peers, Waxahachie, Texas native **John Byron Nelson, Jr.** dominated the PGA tour from 1942 to 1946. In that five-year stretch, he finished in the top 10 in 65 consecutive golf tournaments, winning 34 times with 16 runner-up positions. The Associated Press Male Athlete of the Year in 1944 and 1945, Nelson produced his greatest golf season in 1945. In that magical year, Lord Byron won 18 times, with 11 victories in a row during one stretch. His 68.33 stroke average was not beaten for 55 years. Nelson grew up with fellow Texas golf legend Ben Hogan. Both caddied at Glen Garden County Club and dueled in the 1927 caddie championship, which Nelson won. He would go on to win the Masters in 1937 and 1942, the U.S. Open in 1939 and the PGA Championship in 1940 and 1945. After retiring from competitive golf, he began hosting the Byron Nelson Tournament. Fellow golfing great Ken Venturi once said, "You can always argue who was the greatest golfer, but Byron is the finest gentleman the game has ever known."

NEWELL, PETE: 118, 119

When it comes to working with the National Basketball Association's big men, **Pete Newell** is considered the dean of center instruction and is affectionately considered America's "Basketball Guru." As a coach with the University of San Francisco, Michigan State, and UC Berkeley, Newell compiled a 234-123 record from 1946 to 1960. The master tactician guided the California Golden Bears to consecutive NCAA championship appearances (1959 and 1960), claiming the title in 1959 and earning honors as National Coach of the Year in 1960. Newell coached the 1960 U.S. men's Olympic basketball team, leading future Hall of Famers Jerry West, Jerry Lucas, Oscar Robertson, and Walt Bellamy to gold in Rome. Capturing Olympic gold gave him the amateur triple crown (National Invitational Tournament in 1949, NCAA title, and gold medal). Newell went on to serve as Cal's athletic director from 1960 to 1968 as well as general manager of both the San Diego/Houston Rockets (1968-72) and the Los Angeles Lakers (1972-1976). The coach even squeezed in one season playing minor league baseball at Pine Bluff, Arkansas, in the Class C Cotton States League. His .217 batting average convinced him to return to hoops.

NICKLAUS, JACK: 104, 111

Jack Nicklaus grabbed the PGA tour by the throat in the early 1960s and did not let go until two decades later. His career includes 73 PGA tour victories, a record 18 major titles, eight Champions Tour majors, two U.S. amateur titles (1959 and 1961), and an individual National Collegiate Athletic Association championship at Ohio State University. Nicklaus excelled when it mattered most, capturing the Masters Tournament an amazing six times with a run that began in 1965 and concluded with his final appearance in the fabled green jacket in 1986. His reputation as one of the greatest golfers of all time, if not the greatest, was cemented by his stellar competition, which included Arnold Palmer, Gary Player, Lee Trevino, Johnny Miller, and Tom Watson. A prolific golf course designer, he is the architect of more than 62 courses around the world. Yet despite all the accolades (*Sports Illustrated* Athlete of the Decade for the 1970s) and professional triumphs (113 victories), Nicklaus remains a family man supremely proud of his children and grandchildren.

NEIKRO, PHIL: 81, 90

Phil Neikro is generally credited as the best knuckleball pitcher ever. His statistics show his greatness. He played 24 seasons, mostly for the Milwaukee and Atlanta Braves, and has a lifetime record of 318-274, including a record 121 wins after age 40. He won five Gold Glove awards and hurled a no-hitter against the San Diego Padres in 1973. "Knucksie," as Neikro was called, twice led the National League in wins, posting a personal-best year in 1969 with 23 wins and a 2.57 ERA that helped the Braves capture the National League West title. Elected to the Hall of Fame in 1997, Neikro managed the all-women Colorado Silver Bullets baseball team for a time. His brother, National League Cy Young Award winner Joe, was also an excellent knuckleball pitcher, and several times during their careers they played on the same team.

NORMAN, GREG: 107, 112

The Great White Shark, as Australia native **Greg Norman** has come to be known, ruled the world of golf in the late 1980s and 1990s. Player of the Year in 1995, Norman held the world number one ranking four times between 1986 and 1990 and again in 1995. In one stretch, he was number one in the world for 331 weeks. Norman, known for his booming drives and all-or-nothing approach, won the 1986 and 1993 British Open tournaments. He became the first professional golfer to surpass $10 million in career earnings while capturing a total of 20 PGA wins and 17 on the European tour. However, he never won a major tournament in the United States and is one of only two golfers to lose playoffs in all four majors. Norman has also enjoyed enormous financial success off the course with the marketing of his "Shark" line of golf apparel and his design of golf courses.

O'DELL, NANCY: 49, 55

Nancy O'Dell brings looks, charm, and a reporter's savvy to her anchor post on the award-winning *Access Hollywood*. O'Dell, who graduated summa cum laude from Clemson University, has become the entertainment event hostess. She covers the

Oscar, Emmy, Grammy, and Golden Globe award shows. She also contributes to NBC's *Today Show* and *Dateline*, and hosted the 2004 Miss USA Pageant.

PALMER, ARNOLD: 100, 109

Golf had seen great players before **Arnold Palmer** arrived on the scene in the late 1950s, but no one had ever electrified the galleries and made the country club sport as riveting as The King. Arnie's Army, as his animated fans became known, raced across America's golf courses and turned on their black-and-white television sets to follow their hero's latest Sunday afternoon charge for a PGA title. Born in Latrobe, Pennsylvania in 1929, Palmer scored the first of his 61 PGA victories at the 1955 Canadian Open. He would go on to capture seven major championships—the 1958, 1960, 1962, and 1964 Masters, the 1960 U.S. Open, and the 1961 and 1962 British Opens. With the help of his business manager, Mark McCormack, Palmer parlayed his golf success into a variety of business opportunities off the course, including commercials for automobiles and motor oil. He is also the owner of two country clubs (Latrobe and Bay Hill in Orlando, Florida), a golf course designer, an author, and the marketer of a signature clothing line. Palmer's down-to-earth persona and friendly air made him the face and voice of golf for the second half of the twentieth century.

PALMER, JIM: 80

It was the Baltimore Orioles' good fortune that the Seattle Pilots bypassed a "hurting" **Jim Palmer** in the 1969 expansion draft. Palmer, the youngest pitcher ever to toss a World Series shutout when he beat the Los Angeles Dodgers at age 20 in 1966, went on to win three Cy Young Awards and election to the Baseball Hall of Fame. He was known for his smooth delivery, blazing fastball, and hard curve. Palmer dominated the American League in the 1970s, winning 20 or more games in eight out of nine years. He won World Series games in three different decades (1966, 1970, 1983) on his way to posting 268 career wins and owning nearly every Orioles pitching record. After retiring in 1984, Palmer pursued his broadcasting career with ABC and the local Baltimore station. The only pitch many women ever saw Palmer throw was for Jockey underwear. He appeared in ads in Jockey briefs and was a company spokesman for 20 years, donating his royalties from the famous Jockey ads to the Cystic Fibrosis Foundation.

PERABO, PIPER: 47

A breakout lead role in the hit movie *Coyote Ugly* put New Jersey native **Piper Perabo** on the Hollywood map.

As young songwriter Violet "Jersey" Sanford, Perabo's character never gives up on her dream of being a successful songwriter. The film, based around a legendary New York City bar, Hogs and Heifers, gave rise to a Coyote Ugly bar in the Las Vegas hotel, New York, New York. The Toms River High School (1994) and Ohio University (1998) graduate also appeared in *Cheaper By The Dozen* as one of actor Steve Martin's older children.

PRESTON, KELLY: 45

Born Kelly Kamalelehua Palzis in Hawaii, actress **Kelly Preston** broke into show business, fittingly, in a 1980 *Hawaii Five-O* episode on television. The 5-foot-7 Preston leaped into stardom opposite Arnold Schwarzenegger in the 1988 Ivan Reitman comedy hit, *Twins.* Preston also scored big in two 1990s sports movies. She was the ultra-aggressive fiancée in *Jerry Maguire* (1996), and the sexy single mom in *For Love of the Game* (1999). Now, as the mother of two children with husband John Travolta, Preston has settled into more "Mom" roles in *Jack Frost* and *The Cat in the Hat.*

RAITT, JOHN: 45

The late **John Raitt** defined Broadway's leading man in the 1940s and 1950s when he starred in such classics as *Carousel, Oklahoma!,* and *The Pajama*

Game. He later starred in the film version of *The Pajama Game*, featuring his signature song, "Hey There." In 1957, he starred opposite Mary Martin in *Annie Get Your Gun*, which turned into an NBC special later that year. To a younger generation, the 6-foot-2 Raitt was known as the father of Grammy Award singer Bonnie Raitt. The father and daughter Raitts performed a few songs together on the 1995 album, *John Raitt: The Broadway Legend.* An athlete in high school, Raitt set several California records in the javelin, shot-put, and discus events before attending the University of Southern California on a track scholarship. Raitt never stopped performing on stage, boasting a career that spanned six decades.

REMINI, LEAH: 65, 67

After years of bit parts in hit television comedies, from *Who's the Boss?* to *Cheers*, **Leah Remini** scored as the brash-talking Carrie Heffernan in the CBS hit show, *The King of Queens*. It was a role the Brooklyn-born Remini seemed destined to fill. Playing off Kevin James' physical comedy and the brilliance of the legendary Jerry Stiller, Remini became the sounding board for middle-class housewives. With that success came a part in the film, *Old School.*

RETTON, MARY LOU: 121, 122

Mary Lou Retton, the 4-foot-9 gym-

nast from Fairmont, West Virginia, became the darling of the 1984 Summer Olympics in Los Angeles. Hollywood could not have written a more fitting script as the 16-year-old nailed a score of 10 in her final event, the vault, to secure the women's gymnastics' all-around gold medal. Retton also won two silver and two bronze medals in individual and team competition. Retton-mania landed her on the cover of the Wheaties cereal box, and *Sports Illustrated* named her "Sportswoman of the Year" for 1984. That same year, the Associated Press awarded her the title "Amateur Athlete of the Year." In 1993, an Associated Press national survey named her the "Most Popular Athlete in America," and in 1997 she was elected to the International Gymnastics Hall of Fame. Retton continues speaking around the world and appearing on television as a sports commentator. She has appeared in four movies, including a cameo role in the Bill Murray holiday hit, *Scrooged.*

RICKLES, DON: 41

The king of insults, **Don Rickles** boosted his rise to fame through a chance encounter with legendary crooner Frank Sinatra in 1957. At the Slate Brothers' nightclub in Hollywood, Rickles was working the stage when Sinatra strolled in. The then-unknown comic eyed Sinatra in the crowd and shouted, "I just saw your movie, *The Pride and the Passion*, and I want to tell you, the cannon's acting was great. Make yourself at home, Frank. Hit somebody." Sinatra doubled over with laughter and Rickles was a made entertainer. He was a comic in Las Vegas for much of the 1960s and became a favorite of *Tonight Show* host Johnny Carson because of the sharp barbs he delivered in staccato fashion. His own ABC television show and a top-selling comedy record, *Hello, Dummy!*, further catapulted Rickles to fame in 1968. Children know Rickles as the voice of the pig in the *Toy Story* movies.

RICHARDSON, BOBBY : 87

Bobby Richardson starred as the New York Yankees' second baseman from 1955 to 1966, an era when the Bronx Bombers were nearly automatic entrants in each year's World Series. Richardson's Yankees captured the American League pennant in seven of his first eight big-league seasons. In 1959 and 1962, Richardson—a lifetime .266 hitter—batted .301 and .302. In 1962, he led the league in hits with 209. The seven-time All-Star captured five Gold Gloves (1961-1965) for his slick fielding and was the 1960 World Series' most valuable player despite the Yankees' loss to the Pittsburgh Pirates. At the prime of his career in 1966, the 31-year-old Richardson hung up his glove and spikes to spend more time with his family. He eventually became the head baseball coach at the University of South Carolina and turned the Gamecocks into a national contender.

RIPKEN, CAL, JR.: 84, 90

On the way to playing in a Major League Baseball record 2,632 consecutive games (May 30, 1982 to September 20, 1998), **Cal Ripken, Jr.**, produced Hall of Fame numbers which earned him two American League Most Valuable Player Awards (1983 and 1991) as well as a 1983 World Championship ring with his hometown Baltimore Orioles. The Maryland-born Ripken, whose father managed in the Baltimore minor leagues when Cal was growing up, began his streak during his Rookie of the Year season of 1982. At 6-foot-4, 220 pounds, Ripken ushered in a new shortstop era that featured size-and-power at the position. A two-time Gold Glove winner, Ripken committed just three errors in the entire 1990 season, a record that should stand forever at the position. In 1995, Ripken helped restore baseball's strike-tarnished image by surpassing Lou Gehrig's consecutive game streak of 2,130 games. The father of two finished an incredible Orioles career with 3,184 hits, 431 home runs and two All-Star Most Valuable Player

Awards (1991, 2001). Ripken, who played for his father and brother Billy in 1987, now operates Ripken Baseball, which focuses on youth instruction and playing.

ROBERTS, DORIS: 69

Doris Roberts' career in television and movies began in 1961 with a role in the movie, *Something Wild*. But it was her performance as comedian Ray Romano's mom in the television show *Everybody Loves Raymond* (1996-2005) that etched her in the public's consciousness. A versatile actress, the four-time Emmy Award-winning Roberts also scored successes in television with work on *The Mary Tyler Moore Show*, *Mary Hartman, Mary Hartman*, *Soap*, and *Remington Steele*. Roberts' work in Broadway theater includes *The Time of Your Life* (1955) and *Last of the Red Hot Lovers* (1969). Some of her better-known films include *The Taking of Pelham One Two Three*, in which she starred with Walter Matthau, and *The Rose*, in which she played the mother of the title character, played by Bette Midler.

ROBINSON, BROOKS: 80, 90

Brooks Robinson, third baseman for the Baltimore Orioles, was known as "The Human Vacuum Cleaner" for his remarkable fielding skills (16 straight Gold Glove Awards). The Arkansas-born Robinson captured the 1964 American League Most Valuable Player Award and led the Orioles to their first World Series title in 1966 when the team beat the Los Angeles Dodgers in four straight games. He hit a home run off Don Drysdale in his first at-bat. He also was a key factor in the Orioles' 1970 World Series triumph over the Cincinnati Reds with his sparkling play at third base. Elected to the Baseball Hall of Fame on his first ballot (92 percent of votes) in 1983, Robinson provided color commentary for Orioles television for many years. In 1999, he was selected to the All-Century Team that honored the 25 best baseball players of the twentieth century. Off the field, Robinson was known for his charm and friendliness to his fans.

ROGERS, FRED: 44, 60

No television personality meant more to generations of children than the late **Fred Rogers**. The man with the calm voice, cardigan sweater, tennis shoes, and wonderful neighborhood set a TV standard that may never be duplicated. His PBS show, *Mister Rogers' Neighborhood*, captured every major television award, from the Emmy to the prestigious Peabody. He was also inducted into the Broadcasting Hall of Fame. Rogers taught young children to like themselves, assuring them that they all were special. Born in 1928 in

Latrobe, Pennsylvania, Rogers began his PBS affiliation in 1953 with *The Children's Corner* on Pittsburgh's WQED. In 1966, *Mister Rogers' Neighborhood* was born. Amazingly in an age of commercialism, Rogers refused to capitalize on the success of his show; he turned down commercial appearances and limited marketing to *Neighborhoo*d products — books, videos, and a few basic toys.

ROMNEY, MITT: 18, 24, 32

Born into politics as the son of George Romney, the three-term Michigan governor, **Mitt Romney** graduated from Brigham Young University in 1971 and received business and law degrees from Harvard University in 1975. After a successful career in venture capitalism, the Republican unsuccessfully challenged Ted Kennedy for his Senate seat in 1994. From 1999 to 2002, Romney served as president and CEO of the Salt Lake Organizing Committee. He is credited with coming to the rescue of the 2002 Winter Olympics, erasing its large deficit and restoring its reputation after it was mired in controversy. He was elected governor of Massachusetts in 2002.

ROSEN, AL: 92, 95

As the Cleveland Indians' third baseman, **Al Rosen** was key to the Tribe's upswing in the 1950s. The University of Florida graduate became a starter in 1950 for Cleveland and began a remarkable hitting tear that saw the slugger average 31 home runs and 114 runs batted in during five seasons. In 1953, Rosen's finest season, he came within a whisker of capturing the rare triple crown, leading the American League in home runs (43) and runs batted in (145). However, his .336 batting average fell one point short of the .337 average posted by the Washington Senators' Mickey Vernon. Nicknamed "Flip," Rosen ended his playing years in 1956 with the Indians and began a successful front-office career that saw him serve as team president of the New York Yankees and general manager of the San Francisco Giants.

RUETTIGER, "RUDY": 102

Daniel "Rudy" Ruettiger's name will not appear among the Notre Dame football greats, but the grit and determination which led to his brief appearance on the football field were such an inspiration that Hollywood turned his story into the hit movie, *Rudy*. Ruettiger was an undersized prep star at Illinois' Joliet Catholic High School who battled dyslexia and doubting Thomases. Nobody, parents and teachers included, believed he could attain his dreams of attending the University of Notre Dame and becoming a member of the Fighting Irish powerhouse football team. Rudy's poor high school grades were even more of a hindrance to his goals than his 5-foot-6, 165-pound frame. But two years of hard work at neighboring Holy Cross Junior College paid dividends and, on his final try, Rudy was accepted as a student at Notre Dame in 1974. Then he set out to make the football squad. His heart and never-quit attitude won over a few coaches. But he never saw action until his final home game as a senior. Rudy was sent onto the field in the waning seconds and recorded a quarterback sack as time expired. He was carried off the field on his teammates' shoulders. He has since received many honors, including an honorary doctorate from Our Lady of Holy Cross College and the Distinguished American Award from President George W. Bush. Today, Rudy is co-author of several books and a sought-after motivational speaker who delivers his message of triumph over adversity to international corporate audiences as well as school children, university students, and professional athletes.

RYUN, JIM: 27

A U.S. representative from Kansas since 1996, **Jim Ryun** rose to prominence as the fastest high school and U.S. miler ever. He established a record 3-minute, 51-second mark in 1967 in Bakersfield, California. Congressman Ryun, along with sons Ned and Drew, is the author of *Heroes Among Us*, a book about people who performed courageous acts under trying circumstances.

SANDERS, SUMMER: 70

An Olympic gold medalist swimmer who parlayed her athletic success into a television career co-hosting NBA *Inside Stuff* with Ahmad Rashad, **Summer Sanders** continues to keep several paddles in the water. Author of the book *Champions Are Raised, Not Born*, California-born Sanders has covered every aspect of men's and women's professional basketball, as well as reporting at the Olympics. At the 1992 Summer Olympics in Barcelona, she finished as the most decorated American by winning two golds, a silver, and a bronze medal in swimming. During her two years at Stanford University, the 5-foot-9 Sanders captured six individual NCAA titles, four relay championships, back-to-back NCAA Swimmer of the Year awards, and helped lead the Cardinal to the 1992 NCAA title. When not covering sports, Sanders serves as an ambassador for the United Nations Children's Fund, speaking with children around the world.

SCHWARTZ, SHERWOOD: 50

Many of today's adults spent countless hours as children entertained by the creations of television producer **Sherwood Schwartz**. *Gilligan's Island*, for which he co-wrote the theme song, and *The Brady Bunch* were the two most memorable shows, but the Emmy Award-winning Schwartz has written, re-written, or produced more than 700 television programs. In Gilligan's Island, he named the Skipper's ship the *S.S. Minnow* as a jab at then-Federal Communications Commission Chairman Newton N. Minow, who gave a blistering speech to the National Association of Broadcasters in 1961 in which he referred to television as "a vast wasteland."

SEDAKA, NEIL: 51, 60, 61

A prolific songwriter and pop singer, **Neil Sedaka** topped the charts with such hits as "Oh, Carol," "Calendar Girl," "Happy Birthday Sweet Sixteen," "Next Door to an Angel," and "Breaking Up Is Hard To Do." Sedaka even re-released "Breaking Up Is Hard To Do" as a ballad in the 1970s. It reached Number One on the *Billboard* charts and gave Sedaka the unique honor of having the same song, sung differently by the same star, reach the Top 10 twice. A member of the Songwriters' Hall of Fame, Sedaka has written more than 1,000 songs. Along with his partner and friend Howard Greenfield, he helped establish the "Brill Building Sound" of the late 1950s and early 1960s when they signed with Don Kirshner and Al Nevins at Aldon Music.

SHARMAN, BILL: 93

Bill Sharman is enshrined in the Basketball Hall of Fame as a player (inducted in 1976) and as a coach (2004). Fittingly, he won NBA championships as both player (Boston Celtics) and coach (Los Angeles Lakers). He also guided the American Basketball Association's Utah Stars to a 1971 championship and was at the helm in directing the Lakers to a record 33 straight victories in 1972. Sharman earned 15 varsity letters at Porterville (California) High School and served in the U.S. Navy before starring at the University of Southern California, where he was a first-team All-American in 1950. The eight-time NBA All-Star (most valuable player in 1955) was named to the NBA's 50th Anniversary All-Time Team in 1996. As general manager of the Los Angeles Lakers (1976-1982), Sharman drafted Earvin "Magic" Johnson and James Worthy to help rebuild the Lakers into a dynasty for the 1980s.

SIEVERS, ROY: 87, 94

After being signed by his hometown team, the St. Louis Browns, **Roy Sievers** was the 1949 American League Rookie of the Year (.306 average, 16 home runs, 91 runs batted in).

He went on to become a four-time American League All-Star. Sievers, who spent the bulk of his career with the lowly Washington Senators after they picked him up in 1954, had a lifetime batting average of .267 with 318 home runs and 1,147 runs batted in. Sievers put together a remarkable run from 1954 to 1962 as he never hit less than 21 home runs and surpassed 90 RBI seven times. In 1957, Sievers' finest season, the Senator batted .301 with a league-leading 42 home runs and 114 RBI.

SMITH, KEVIN: 52

Kevin Smith burst onto the cinema scene in 1994 with his cult hit, *Clerks*. Filmed after hours in a convenience store where Smith was employed, the New Jersey native's movie spoke to the grunge generation as no other director's film had. Smith had to sell his prized comic book collection to fund his low-budget, independent movie. When it became a hit, he bought all his comic books back. *Clerks* captured the top honor at the Sundance Film Festival. His sequel, *Mallrats* (1995), helped establish his long-term relationship with actors Ben Affleck and Jason Lee, who would star in *Chasing Amy* (1997). Smith has since directed *Dogm*a (1999), *Jay and Silent Bob Strike Back* (2001), and *Jersey Girl* (2004). Smith has also appeared in every film he has made

and his love of comics led him to writing for Marvel (*Daredevil*) and DC (*Green Arrow*).

SMOTHERS, TOM AND DICK: 37

In the evolution of topical comedy television shows, *The Smothers Brothers Comedy Hour*, featuring real-life brothers **Tom and Dick Smothers**, bridged the gap between Sid Caesar's celebrated shows of the 1950s and NBC's *Saturday Night Live* in the mid-1970s. At the time, however, its frequent digs at the dominant institutions of the day and sketches about sensitive issues (drugs, the Vietnam war) made the show one of the most controversial in television history. Public battles occurred over taste and censorship until CBS threw the show off the air in 1969, two years after its 1967 debut. Before their TV shows, the Smothers brothers blended perfectly timed humor and music in a unique club act that debuted in 1959 at the famed Purple Onion in San Francisco. Less than two years later, the Brothers appeared on Jack Paar's late-night television talk show and the San Jose State University grads were rocketing to stardom. When not touring the country with their act, the brothers own and operate Remrick Ridge Vineyard in Kenwood, California.

SPENCE, GERRY: 21

A country lawyer with an unbeatable

record, **Gerry Spence** may be the master of the oral argument. He has never lost a jury trial or a criminal case. In fact, one of his 13 books, *How to Argue and Win Every Time* (1995), was a national bestseller. Born and raised in Wyoming, Spence graduated cum laude from the University of Wyoming School of Law in 1952. He achieved fame with impressive courtroom wins, including the successful representation of the estate of Karen Silkwood, an anti-nuclear activist who was killed in an automobile accident under suspicious circumstances. The $10.5 million judgment for Silkwood's children garnered major headlines. As a young lawyer, Spence worked as a prosecutor and eventually drifted into defense work with an impressive list of insurance company clients. But the work took its toll and Spence decided to go in a new direction representing people. To this day, he has not represented another corporation, insurance company, bank, or big business.

STEINBERG, LEIGH: 28, 30

National Football League superagent **Leigh Steinberg** was the inspiration behind the Tom Cruise character in the award-winning *Jerry Maguire*. Steinberg's career as an agent began in 1974 when he negotiated what was then the largest NFL rookie contract, for University of California quarterback Steve Bartkowski. Success came quickly and he has represented more than 150 professional athletes, including such A-list quarterbacks as Steve Young, Warren Moon, Ben Rothlisberger, Troy Aikman, Drew Bledsoe, and Jeff George. Steinberg has represented the number one pick in the NFL draft a record eight times. He has served as a consultant on the movies *Jerry Maguire*, *On Any Given Sunday*, and *Arli$$*. What separates Steinberg from others in the agent field is his strong desire for the athletes to make a positive contribution to society. He insists that each contract his players sign includes a clause requiring them to give back to the community. Steinberg's clients have donated more than $60 million to hundreds of charities and scholarships nationwide.

STEINEM, GLORIA: 19

Gloria Steinem, perhaps the country's best known feminist writer and activist, first came to the public's attention with her 1963 *Show* article, "I Was a Playboy Bunny." In 1972, Steinem was a founding editor of *Ms. Magazine*, where she served as editor for 15 years, then as a columnist and finally as a consulting editor. In 1983, she published *Outrageous Acts and Everyday Rebellions*, followed in 1986 by *Marilyn*, and *Revolution from Within* in 1992.

THOMPSON, LEA: 51

A ballet dancer who starred in *Jaws 3-D*, **Lea Thompson** came to the attention of the boys in the 1983 film, *All The Right Moves*. Next, she struck solid gold costarring with Michael J. Fox in the *Back to the Future* trilogy, proving that comedy comes just as easily to her as drama. Thompson captured the teen angst of trying to stay with the in-crowd with her turn in John Hughes' *Some Kind of Wonderful*. Besides movies, Thompson has starred in the NBC hit show, *Caroline in the City* and on stage in the musical, *Cabaret*, and the drama, *Bus Stop*.

THOMSON, BOBBY: 86

New York Giants legend **Bobby Thomson** achieved baseball immortality with one swing of the bat. His three-run blast in the bottom of the ninth inning gave the Giants the 1951 National League pennant over their bitter cross-town rivals, the Brooklyn Dodgers. "The Shot Heard Round the World" was all the more sweet because it capped an amazing comeback for a team that was 13 ^{1}/2 games out of first place in mid-August. Thomson skipping home after his historic homer as Giants announcer Russ Hodges repeatedly screamed "The Giants win the pennant!" is one of the most often replayed moments in sports history. The greatest major leaguer to come from Scotland (born in Glasgow in

1923), Thomson played from 1946 to 1960. From 1949 to 1953, "The Staten Island Scot" hit at least 24 home runs and drove in 100 or more runs in four of the five seasons. A lifetime .270 hitter, Thomson finished with 264 home runs and 1,026 runs batted in. Signed by the Giants in 1942, Thomson missed three full seasons while serving in the U.S. Army during World War II. His career ended on July 26, 1960 when he was released by the Baltimore Orioles.

TREVINO, LEE: 108, 112

Golf's true Cinderella story belongs to **Lee Trevino**. Raised in a run-down shack near Glen Lakes Country Club in Dallas, the self-taught Trevino went from collecting lost golf balls to caddying, then on to winning the 1968 U.S. Open at Oak Hill Golf Club after just one year on the PGA tour. While his unorthodox swing provided fodder for golf commentators, Trevino charged ahead with success, winning 29 times between 1968 and 1984. During a four-week period in 1971, he won the U.S. Open, the Canadian Open, and the British Open. Trevino even pulled a miracle comeback at the age of 44 in 1984 with his victory in the prestigious PGA Championship. After joining the PGA Senior Tour (now the Champions Tour) in 1990, Trevino captured another 29 titles. His quick wit and gamesmanship have always made him a fan favorite out on the course.

TRUCKS, VIRGIL: 87

One of the best pitchers of the late 1940s and 1950s, Detroit Tigers fireballer **Virgil Trucks** led the American League in strikeouts and shutouts in 1949. Three years later, he became one of only four pitchers in baseball history to toss two no-hitters in a single season. Like many players of his generation, Trucks may have lost the prime years of his 1941-1958 baseball career serving in the United States military during World War II. An All-Star pitcher in 1949 and 1954, Trucks is considered one of the best pitchers not enshrined in the Baseball Hall of Fame.

TURNER, MORRIE: 62, 75

Morrie Turner's "Wee Pals" cartoon strip became a must-read for many kids during the 1970s because Turner made sure to include a Rainbow Coalition of children when he created it in 1965. His goal was to create a world without prejudice, where differences of race, religion, gender, and physical and mental ability are embraced rather than scorned. Turner's "Wee Pals" began with just five newspapers. It took the tragic assassination of Martin Luther King, Jr. for "Wee Pals" to gain wide acceptance. Within three month's of King's death, the strip appeared in more than 100 newspapers.

UEBERROTH, PETER: 19

Time Magazine's 1984 Man of the Year for leading the Los Angeles Olympic Organizing Committee to the most successful Summer Games in modern history, **Peter Ueberroth** has a knack for turning troubled organizations into profitable business ventures. Ueberroth rescued the LAOOC from bankruptcy and produced a hefty $222 million surplus that funds youth and sports programs to this day. Riding a successful wave, Ueberroth accepted Major League Baseball's offer to become its commissioner. In 1984, 22 baseball teams were bleeding financial losses. By the time Ueberroth stepped down in 1989, his no-nonsense style of leadership left every team with a profit by season's end. Ueberroth is part of the joint venture that purchased California's Pebble Beach golf course from a Japanese corporation and he serves as co-chairman of the Pebble Beach Company. He got his business start by creating First Travel Corporation in 1962. When he sold it in 1980, it was the second largest travel business in North America. He is a San Jose State University graduate.

UNITAS, JOHNNY: 95, 105

A ninth-round draft pick out of Louisville by the Pittsburgh Steelers in 1955, the late **Johnny Unitas** was dropped from the team before flinging a single pass. Banished to the hard semi-pro leagues, he played that season for $6 a game. In 1956, he signed with the Baltimore Colts for $17,000. Two years later, he introduced the "Two-Minute Drill" to America. He completed four passes in the final 90 seconds of the NFL Championship game against the New York Giants to set up a game-tying field goal with seven seconds left. Baltimore then won the NFL's first overtime title game on his pass that capped an 80-yard touchdown drive. Unitas retired in 1974 after one season with the San Diego Chargers. During his 18-year career, the two-time MVP recipient played in 10 Pro Bowls and led the Colts to three championships. In all, he left the game with 22 records, including most yards gained passing (40,239), most completed passes (2,830), and most touchdown passes (290). He was inducted into the Pro Football Hall of Fame in 1979. In 2000, he was voted "The Greatest Player in the First Fifty Years of Pro Football."

VAN PATTEN, DICK: 51

Best known as columnist Tom Bradford on ABC's hit show *Eight Is Enough*, **Dick Van Patten** is a former child actor who spoofed Hollywood's temptations in *Dickie Roberts: Former Child Star* (2003). He was also seen on the big screen in *Gus* (1976), *Freaky Friday* (1976), and *The Shaggy D.A.*

(1976). Van Patten's tennis pal Mel Brooks cast him in *High Anxiety* (1977), *Spaceballs* (1987), and *Robin Hood: Men in Tights* (1993). Throughout the 1970s and 1980s, Van Patten found plenty of work in television, popping up five times as a guest star on ABC's *The Love Boat*. Acting is a family business for the Van Pattens. Sons Nels, James, and Vincent are actors, his sister is actress Joyce Van Patten, and his half-brother is director Timothy Van Patten.

VENTURI, KEN: 108

Ken Venturi, the 1964 U.S. Open champion, shifted from a great playing career in his mid-30s into a successful 35-year broadcasting career. Not bad for a man who took to golf's solitude to escape his stammering problem. Helped by golf legends Byron Nelson and Ben Hogan, Venturi was a force in the game from 1957 to 1964. He hobnobbed with Hollywood's elite, at one time rooming with Frank Sinatra. Venturi, who turned down a contract from the New York Yankees at 18, survived record temperatures and dehydration to best Tommy Jacobs in the 1964 U.S. Open. Two years later, carpal tunnel syndrome prematurely ended his golf career, but gave birth to the golf analyst.

VINTON, BOBBY: 41, 76

Dubbed by *Billboard* magazine "the

all-time most successful love singer of the Rock Era," **Bobby Vinton** dominated the 1960s hit charts with "Roses Are Red," "Blue Velvet," and "Mr. Lonely." The singing success of The Polish Prince (also the title of his autobiography) would lead to a hit television variety special for CBS in the 1970s and an acting career that saw him appear with John Wayne in *Big Jake* (1971) and *The Train Robbers* (1973). Vinton moved his act to Branson, Missouri, where he built the Bobby Vinton Blue Velvet Theatre, and performs many songs from his dozen gold records. Today, he also performs in Las Vegas, Atlantic City, and other venues around the world. An accomplished musician who can play piano, clarinet, saxophone, trumpet, drums, and oboe, the Pittsburgh-born and-raised Vinton helped finance his own education at his hometown Duquesne University with his rock band gigs.

VITALE, DICK: 48

Nobody loves college basketball more than Dick Vitale, ESPN's lead college analyst. A former successful head coach at the University of Detroit, the Seton Hall graduate took an unsuccessful stab at the NBA with the Detroit Pistons before finding a home on the fledgling all-sports network. Imitated but never duplicated, Vitale's lingo ("Diaper Dandy," "Dipsey-Doo-Dunkeroo"), matches the intensity level of most college basketball games.

WALKER, HERSCHEL: 101

Combining power and speed, **Herschel Walker** starred at the University of Georgia for three seasons, leading the Bulldogs to a national title and capturing the Heisman Trophy in 1982. In 1983, he gave up his final year of collegiate eligibility and turned professional, joining the New Jersey Generals of the short-lived United States Football League. Walker earned Most Valuable Player honors and set the single-season pro football rushing record (2,411 yards). After his first pro season, he finished his bachelor of science degree in criminal justice at the University of Georgia. Walker joined the Dallas Cowboys in 1986, led the National Football League in rushing, and earned All-Pro honors. He moved to the Minnesota Vikings as starting running back in 1989 and joined the Philadelphia Eagles in 1992. He returned to the Cowboys in 1996 and retired from the NFL in 1997. Walker gained more yards than anyone in professional football history, counting his seasons in both the NFL and USFL. He finished his professional career with a total of 8,225 yards and 61 rushing touchdowns. He also caught 512 passes for 4,859 yards and 21 scores. Walker was elected to the

National Football Foundation and College Hall of Fame in 1999.

WALKER, MORT: 40

Creator of the long-running comic strip "Beetle Bailey," Mort Walker's career surpasses 50 years. Born in 1923, he had his first comic published at the age of 11, but cartooning did not come as easily later in life. After a four-year military stint, Walker worked as an editor of three Dell magazines. His first 200 cartoons were rejected, but he never gave up. In 1950, King Features picked up "Beetle Bailey" for syndication, with Beetle a college flake who did not land in the Army until 1951. In 1954, Walker co-created the comic strip "Hi and Lois." In 1970, his addition of Lt. Jack Flap made "Beetle Bailey" the first strip to integrate a black character into a white cast. "Beetle Bailey" runs in more than 1,800 newspapers.

WATKINS, DONALD V.: 20, 27

Donald Watkins was one of the first five African-Americans to enroll at the University of Alabama School of Law in 1970. He later won 37 out of 38 lawsuits on behalf of the city of Birmingham, Alabama during the 1980s and 1990s. The civil rights attorney turned banker/energy-industry investor is rumored to have amassed a $1.5 billion fortune, but he refuses to tout his wealth or ask to be placed on any money lists. He has made attempts to purchase the Minnesota Twins and Anaheim Angels baseball teams, but neither has come to fruition.

WATSON, TOM: 106, 111

Mention **Tom Watson** to golf enthusiasts and two images come to mind. First is the British Open, which Watson won an amazing five times. Second is the chip shot for a birdie at Pebble Beach's 17th green that propelled him past Jack Nicklaus to win the 1982 U.S. Open. Watson was a successful golfer at Stanford University prior to joining the professional tour in 1971. In 1974, after Byron Nelson met with the struggling Watson to discuss his game, an unbelievable run began that would launch Watson to the top tier of the golf world in the 1970s and 1980s. Watson was the leading money winner on the tour five times, amassing 36 victories between 1974 and 1984. In addition to his five British Open wins, Watson won the Masters Tournament twice and the U.S. Open once.

WILLIAMS, ANDY: 55

Andy Williams made it on stage and television as a gifted crooner who sang the standards. His hit television program, *The Andy Williams Show* (1962-1972), captured three Emmy Awards as Best Musical/Variety Series. Williams will be forever tied to his rendition of "Moon River" as well as his holiday hit, "The Most Wonderful

Time of the Year." He has 18 gold and three platinum albums to his credit. As owner and featured performer at the $12 million, state-of-the-art Andy Williams Moon River Theatre in Branson, Missouri, he continues to delight sold-out audiences.

WINKLER, HENRY: 42, 60

A talented director and Emmy Award-winning producer, **Henry Winkler** is best known as the cool, leather-jacketed Arthur "Fonzie" Fonzarelli on ABC's *Happy Days* (1974-1984). The two-time Golden Globe winner and Yale School of Drama graduate also starred in the comedy flick, *Night Shift* (1982). A successful children's author and television producer, Winkler has appeared in the movie, *Scream* and the television show, *Arrested Development*. His children's books include *Niagara Falls or Does It?* and *I Got a D in Salami*. He has appeared on Broadway in *The Dinner Party.*

WOODEN, JOHN: 103, 117

One of the all-time greatest college basketball coaches, **John Wooden** began his hardwood experience as a three-time all-American player at Purdue University (1930-32) that included being named Player of the Year as a senior. Coach Wooden guided the UCLA men's basketball program to a record 10 NCAA championships (including seven in a row) and won 88 consecutive basketball games. Coach Wooden was elected to the Naismith Basketball Hall of Fame as both a player and a coach. His lifetime record of 677-161 (80.5 percent) in 29 years is remarkable. Yet Coach Wooden takes his greatest pride as father of two, grandfather of seven, and great-grandfather of eight. His letter to Nicholas included a copy of the poem by Rev. Claude Wisdom White, Sr., "A Little Fellow Follows Me." Coach Wooden wrote below the White poem: "The original of this was presented to me in 1936 upon the birth of my son and has been kept nearby since then."

WOOTTEN, MORGAN: 117

In 1956, **Morgan Wootten** took the head coaching job at DeMatha High School in Hyattsville, Maryland. After 46 years, Coach Wootten retired with a total of five national titles, the best winning percentage of any basketball coach (.869), a stretch from 1960-1991 where every senior on the varsity team was offered a college scholarship, and without a losing season (1,274-192). More than a coach, Wootten taught history for 32 years at the all-boys' Catholic high school. In 2000, Coach Wootten was inducted into the Basketball Hall of Fame, later being named the Naismith Award winner as outstanding male preparatory school coach of the twentieth century.

WOUK, HERMAN: 24

Born in New York City, **Herman Wouk** drew on his U.S. Navy service in World War II for his 1951 Pulitzer Prize-winning novel, *The Caine Mutiny*. The book later became the basis for a hit play and movie. World War II also stood as the backdrop for Wouk's two-volume historical novel, *The Winds of War* (1971) and *War and Remembrance* (1975), which became a hit mini-series in the 1970s. Wouk is also the author of *Who'll Stop the Carnival*, which portrayed the ultimate businessman's dream escape to a rum-punch paradise. He teamed up with singer Jimmy Buffett to create a musical of the same name.